Orthodox Christian
Bible Commentary

JAMES
1 PETER
2 PETER

By His Eminence Metropolitan Youssef

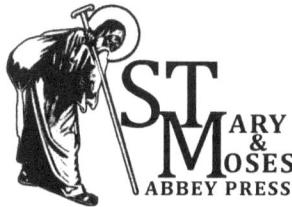

ST MARY
&
MOSES
ABBEY PRESS

Designed & Published by:
St. Mary & St. Moses Abbey Press
101 S Vista Dr., Sandia, TX 78383
stmabbeypress.com

Printed in the United States of America

Library of Congress Control Number: 2020950237

Cover design image photo by Katherine Nawar,
and icon from Bedour Latif and Youssef Nassief.

10   9   8   7   6   5   4   3   2

❧ *Contents* ❧

The Epistle of
James

AUTHOR: St. James. This Epistle was written by Saint James as is made clear in Chapter 1, Verse 1.

PLACE & TIME: The letter may have been written around AD 48. We derive this date because of certain clues. First, James was the head of the Council of Jerusalem and this Council was held in the year AD 49. Since there was no mention of the Jerusalem Conference in this letter, it is considered to have been written beforehand. Additionally, he used the word "synagogue" in the letter. All of this points to the AD 48 date.

With this date in mind, consider that James the son of Zebedee was martyred in AD 44, so that would exclude him from being the author of this letter.

Interestingly, considering this letter to have been written in AD 48 signifies that the Epistle of St. James was the first book written in the New Testament. If asked, what was the first book written in the New Testament, the answer is, "the letter of James." All the other epistles were written after that.

As for the place of writing of this letter, since James the brother of the Lord is the author and was the Bishop of Jerusalem, most likely, he wrote this epistle in Jerusalem.

Who is St. James? There are three men in the Bible who carry the name James. The first one is James the son of Zebedee. He is also the brother of John the Beloved, the author of the Gospel according to St. John, the three letters bearing his name, and the Book of Revelation.

James and John were fishermen, and they were called by the Lord Jesus Christ to be among the twelve disciples.

Although the first martyr in Christianity

was St. Stephen, the first martyr among the twelve disciples was James the son of Zebedee, who was killed by King Herod in AD 44.

James the son of Zebedee is not the author of this Letter.

There are two others to consider. First, we have James the son of Alphaeus, who is also one of the twelve apostles. There is also James, the brother of the Lord. The scholars are divided. Some say these are not two different people but only one person.

In actuality, James the brother of the Lord is different.

Alphaeus is identified with another name: Clopas. Biblical scholars say that this James is the cousin of the Lord and, therefore, is called the brother of the Lord, because he is regarded by some scholars as being the son of the other Mary, who is specifically identified as being the sister of St. Mary the Virgin (Jn 19:25).

Some other scholars contend that James the son of Alphaeus is different than James the brother of the Lord, making them two different people. Moreover, they say the third James, the brother of the Lord, is actually the Lord's cousin, and that he is different from James the son of Alphaeus, who initially did not believe in the Lord, but later believed and became the Bishop of Jerusalem.

James, the brother of the Lord, is the author of this Letter.

If he and James, the son of Alphaeus, are the same person, then James the son of Alphaeus or James the brother of the Lord is the author of this Epistle, but if they are two different persons, then James the brother of the Lord, who later became the Bishop of Jerusalem and also headed the Council of Jerusalem (Acts 15), is the author of this Letter.

Tradition describes James as a man of prayer. As we study his letter, you will notice he emphasizes the importance of prayer. It was said about him that he prayed so much while kneeling on his knees, that his knees became as hard as those of a camel. He was martyred in AD 62.

There are two stories about his martyrdom. One account is that they threw him from a temple, and the other is that they beat him to death by a club.

The story of his martyrdom mentions that he prayed to the Lord Jesus Christ and said, "Lord forgive them for they know not what they do."

In conclusion, the author is James the brother of the Lord, who could also be the son of Alphaeus, the Bishop of Jerusalem.

RECIPIENT OF THIS LETTER

Jews Living Outside Jerusalem

In Chapter 1 Verse 1, the Epistle is addressed "To the twelve tribes who are scattered abroad"—referring to Jews that are living outside of Jerusalem or outside Palestine. Since the various Jewish captivities (e.g. the Babylonian captivity and the Assyrian captivity), many Jews lived outside of Jerusalem, outside of Palestine, and they were scattered to various places.

In this letter, St. James repeated the words "beloved brethren" or "brethren in the Lord" several times, indicating that these were converts to Christianity. In the first century, the word "brother" referred to brothers in the Christian faith, so the word "brethren" means they were Christians. St. James referred to the recipients in this way nineteen times, and one time he called them, "brethren in the Lord."

This is reminiscent of St. Paul's remarks in 1 Corinthians 5. He told the Corinthians not to associate with evildoers, then St. Paul clarified that he did not mean that people refrain from associating with the evildoers of the world, otherwise they would need to leave the world. Instead, what was meant is that if a "brother" is an evildoer, do not associate with him (1 Cor 5:11).

St. James, therefore, indicates that he is addressing the Christians who are of a Jewish background and are scattered outside of Jerusalem.

These Jewish converts to Christianity were quite poor and oppressed for two reasons: the Jews outside of Jerusalem were living among the Pagan Gentiles, and most of the time they were rejected by the Gentiles, additionally, these Jews converted to Christianity, so they were also rejected by the Israelites. That is why their condition was very difficult. This letter indicates that most of them were poor and that rich people oppressed some of them.

Moreover, since this letter was not addressed to a single church or to a single individual like the letters of St. Paul (e.g., he addressed his letters either to the church at Corinth or to the church at Ephesus, or to individuals like Timothy, Titus, Philemon), this letter is part of what are called the "General Letters" or the "Catholic (universal) Epistles." This signifies the letter was not sent to a certain church or to a certain individual. These Catholic Epistles include the Epistles of James, Peter, John, and Jude.

PURPOSE FOR WRITING THIS LETTER

St. James wrote about very practical aspects of Christian life. This letter is the most practical letter. It gives you clear instructions. The whole letter consists of 108 verses. Almost one half of the verses are direct instructions describing what you need to do in a practical way, and for this reason, there is much similarity between this letter and the prophecy of Amos in the Old Testament. That is why some scholars like to call St. James, "The Amos of the New Testament."

We can divide the letter into five messages:

I. **True Religion and Trials, or True Religion Endures Trials.** If you are truly religious, you will endure the trial.

II. **True Religion and Wisdom, or Displays of Wisdom.** If you are truly religious, you will display wisdom.

III. **True Religion is Doing and Not Just Hearing.** If you are truly religious, you will be a doer of the word not only a hearer of the word.

IV. **True Religion is Based on Humility.** If you are truly religious, you will be humble.

V. **True Religion is Blessed through Patience, Prayer, and Love.** If you are truly religious, you will be patient, prayerful, and loving.

Therefore, these are the practical points:

• True religion endures trials.

• True religion makes you a doer of the word not only a hearer.

• True religion displays wisdom.

• True religion is based on humility.

• True religion is blessed through patience, prayer, and love.

OUTLINE OF JAMES

Chapter 1
• Greeting to the twelve tribes (1)
• Profiting from trials (2-8)
• The perspective of rich and poor (9-11)
• Loving God under trials (12-18)
• Qualities needed in trials (19-20)
• Doers, not hearers only (21-27)

Chapter 2
• Beware of personal favoritism (1-13)
• Faith without works is dead (14-26)

Chapter 3
• The untamable tongue (1-12)
• Heavenly verses demonic (13-18)
• Discussion about the Church (14-16)

Chapter 4
• Pride promotes strife (1-6)
• Humility cures worldliness (7-10)
• Do not judge a brother (11-12)
• Do not boast about tomorrow (13-17)

Chapter 5
• Rich oppressors will be judged (1-6)
• Be patient and persevere (7-12)
• Meeting specific needs (13-18)
• Bring back the erring one (19-20)

1

Chapter Outline

Introduction

Chapter 1 begins with the salutation. In verses 2 to 5, St. James explains that trials are opportunities and occasions for us to grow. In order to handle trials, wisdom is needed, which you can receive from the Lord. St. James says we should ask God with faith (5–8).

Recall that most Jews outside of Jerusalem who converted to Christianity were poor and oppressed, so St. James wanted to comfort them (9–11), telling them that the poor are to rejoice in their exaltation. They are exalted because they are heirs of the kingdom of heaven, they are exalted because they are the children of God. Even if they are deprived from financial resources, they should, nonetheless, glory and rejoice in their exaltation, that they will inherit the true richness in heaven. The rich, however, will glory in their humiliation, which will be explained in detail further below.

St. James turns his focus to dealing with temptation, giving practical instructions on how to deal with it (12–15). He also clarifies that if you are tempted, do not say, "I am tempted by God (v 13)," because God is the Father of every good and perfect gift, which comes down from above (16–18).

St. James concludes this chapter by instructing us to be doers of the word, not only hearers.

1:1 James, a bondservant of God and of the Lord Jesus Christ, To the twelve tribes which are scattered abroad: Greetings. In Greek, "bondservant" is translated "slave." In the Jewish tradition there was "a year of release," in which the master releases all the slaves, but if a slave came and said, "I like my master and I want to be his slave the rest of my life," then they would take this slave and pierce his ear, and he would be considered bonded to his master (cf. Exodus 21:5-6).

Although Christ gave us freedom, by our own choice we want to be His slaves, His servants, and His bondservants. "Bondservant," in this sense, means, "I am tied to my master the Lord Jesus

Christ with a bond, and that bond is love. The bond of love has made me, by my own free will, choose to be His slave. I know how much He loves me; He died on the cross for my sake."

That is why instead of simply beginning the epistle with the words, "James, the apostle of the Lord Jesus Christ," he exulted more so in describing himself as "a bondservant," a slave "of God and of the Lord Jesus Christ."

Some scholars have said that because St. James used the term "bondservant" to describe himself, this means he was not an apostle: that is not true. He was an apostle, but used the word "bondservant," as has been explained. Additionally, consider that he was addressing the Israelites, in general, and maybe some of the Jewish people who did not yet believe in Jesus Christ, who had not converted to Christianity, were reading this letter too, so we notice that he omitted the title "apostle" and used the term "bondservant" to remain humble and not be intimidating.

To the twelve tribes, which are scattered abroad: Greetings. Jews outside of Judea were called the "dispersion." This was part of God's plan and economy, to disperse the Jews outside of Jerusalem in order to spread His Name. Those who were scattered abroad preached the word of God all over the world.

1:2 My brethren, count it all joy when you fall into various trials. When people fall into trials, hardship, and tribulation, they usually complain; but, St. James is telling us that we need to rejoice instead of complaining. Why? Rejoice because this is considered a test of your faith, and if you pass the test, you will grow and be strengthened. God allows trials for us to grow through hardship. When you endure trials, you will learn how to be patient, you will gain experience, and at the end, victory. Thus, wise people should rejoice when they fall into various trials.

1:3 knowing that the testing of your faith produces patience. Trials test your faith. If you fall into trials and start to complain, or you accuse God, or you start fighting with others, you are not working through the trial with faith. The test of my faith is measured by my reaction to the situation. Its product should be patience. By enduring trials with patience, we grow and become stronger. Other people who do not endure but rather give up before the end, do not benefit.

That is why in verse 4, he said,

1:4 But let patience have its perfect work. Do you want to be perfect? Do you want to be complete?

Do you want to lack nothing? Be patient to the end. The Lord taught us, "He who endures to the end shall be saved" (Mt 24:13). Those who endure should not be passive but have perfect work. Passive endurance is one who asks, "What can I do? Do I have other options?" The opposite are those who know they have other options, but choose, by their own free will, to endure and be patient to the end.

that you may be perfect and complete, lacking nothing. Patient endurance of trials will make you perfect and complete. When we endure to the end, we will grow in perfection and completion and nothing will be lacking in our lives. In order to understand this concept, which is the total opposite of what the world teaches, you need God's help. You need to know that it is the heavenly wisdom that makes you rejoice in trials, as explained in the next verse.

If you have difficulty in accepting this concept of rejoicing in trials and consider this as nonsense, that is an indication you are lacking wisdom. That leads you then to the solution: wisdom.

1:5 If any of you lacks wisdom, let him ask of God, who gives to all liberally and without reproach, and it will be given to him. If you have difficulty accepting this notion of rejoicing in trials, then get on your knees and ask God to give you His divine wisdom to accept the concept of rejoicing in trials. If you lack wisdom, the wisdom to understand how to "count it all joy when you fall into various trials," ask God for it. He told us, "Ask, and it will be given to you" (Mt 7:7).

God listens to us, and in answer to our prayers, He gives "liberally." He gives liberally with abundance, as we say in the Gregorian Liturgy, that we receive "more than we ask or understand." Unlike some people who when they give, do it with reproach, God gives to us "liberally and without reproach." He never reproaches us on account of our requests, as we often do to one another. He will never reproach us because He loves us, and He gives us with abundance and liberally.

1:6 But let him ask in faith. Many people say, "But I pray and I do not receive: why is that?" That is because you pray without faith. Faith, then, is an essential element for prayers to prevail, to be heard, and to be answered.

with no doubting. If you have doubts, if you doubt the power of God, then you are like Martha and Mary, who doubted Christ's power to raise Lazarus. They thought that God's power was limited to just healing Lazarus. That is why they told Him: "If You had been here, my brother would not have died" (Jn

11:21). In their mind, Lazarus was dead and God could then do nothing.

for he who doubts is like a wave of the sea driven and tossed by the wind. If you doubt the power of God, you will be like the wave of the sea. Sometimes you will go back and forth, "Yes, God can do it; no, God cannot do it. Yes, God will do it; no, God will not do it." Like the wave of the sea, you will be driven (which means from the outside) and tossed (which means from within).

Sometimes doubt comes from the outside, by people who instill doubts in your heart, but also, Satan may instill doubts inside your heart. It may be that the doubts will come from within you; thus, you need to ask in faith without any doubts.

1:7 For let not that man suppose that he will receive anything from the Lord. Every day we receive many good gifts from God. In this verse, when St. James says. "anything," he means anything pertaining to the request that he made of God. So, if you pray with doubts, you will not receive that for which you prayed, and your prayer will not be answered.

1:8 he is a double-minded man,

unstable in all his ways. The term "double-minded" is used to describe one mind that is directed towards God ("Yes, God will listen to me"), and the other mind directed away from God ("God will not listen to me"). Note that "double-minded" here is not hypocrisy, because it refers just to doubt and wavering. It is not that he is convinced with something in his heart but shows something else; that would be hypocrisy and that is not what is meant here. It is doubt, instability, and wavering.

Some people say, "I do not doubt God; I doubt myself, whether I am worthy to receive or not. Yes, I trust that God can raise this dead man, I trust that God can solve my problems, but I do not trust myself because I know that I am not worthy to receive such blessings from God." Therefore, sometimes, we do not doubt God but we doubt our worthiness, and this results in double-mindedness.

1:9 Let the lowly brother glory in his exaltation. God will answer our prayers not because we are worthy, but rather, because He is good and His mercy endures forever. That is the difference between grace and reward. Grace is a free gift given based on the goodness of the giver not on the worthiness of the receiver; reward is based on worthiness. God, however, deals with us through His Grace: "grace and truth came through Jesus Christ" (Jn 1:17); therefore, you should not doubt that God would answer your prayers though you are unworthy.

In the second canticle of the Midnight Praises, we say, "We give thanks to the Lord for He is good and His mercy endures forever." We know, before we pray, that all of us are unworthy; nonetheless, He is great.

His mercy is so rich, His goodness is so rich, and His love is so abundant toward us, that is why we need to rejoice, knowing that God will answer our prayers. This mindset will help you in your double-mindedness. Rejoice and glory because God exalts you. Yes, we know that we are lowly, we know that we are not worthy, but "let the lowly brother glory in his exaltation."

God chose you to be His son and His daughter. None of us are worthy of this, but God exalts us by making us His children and heirs of glory and of the kingdom of heaven. And all these gifts are given to us because of His unconditional love for us, because of His Grace. While unworthy, we are exalted.

1:10 **but the rich in his humiliation, because as a flower of the field he will pass away.** St. James did not say, "the rich brother," but just "the rich." It is very clear that he is speaking about nonbelievers who are rich and oppress the believers.

While the lowly brother glories in his exaltation, the rich, unfortunately, glory and rejoice in things that will later bring their humiliation. That is because they usually glory and put their trust and confidence in riches, not in God; however, the world will pass away and all its treasures (1 Jn 2:17).

A rich believer then should not put their trust in the riches of the world. Rather, he should humble himself before God; otherwise, the rich who glory in riches will pass away "as a flower of the field." This can cause double-mindedness— sometimes trust in God, sometimes not.

1:11 **For no sooner has the sun risen with a burning heat than it withers the grass; its flower falls, and its beautiful appearance perishes. So the rich man also will fade away in his pursuits.** "Sun" refers to trials. If you put your trust in riches, when you fall into hardship or trial, riches will not secure you. It may bring you many things, but it cannot bring you health, for example, or peace and inner joy.

When trials hit, riches will be gone and "its flower falls," and the beautiful appearance perishes. That is what will happen to the rich man who trusts in riches; he will fade away in all his pursuits. When the sun of trials rises with a burning heat, the rich will not be able to rejoice; in the midst of their various pleasures, they will fade away.

1:12 Blessed is the man who endures temptation; for when he has been approved, he will receive the crown of life which the Lord has promised to those who love Him. St James is referring back to the notion of patient endurance to the end (v. 4–5, above). He that endures and continues faithfully shall obtain the crown of life. Therefore, there is a special blessing when you are patient and endure while still here on earth. When you are approved, when you pass the test of faith, you will receive the crown of life in heaven, and this crown is promised to those who love Him.

Some people will not endure to the end and they will accuse God and blame Him for the trials they faced; but some people will endure to the end. Such endurance proves our love. If you read 1 Corinthians 13, it says that love "endures all things," so without love, you cannot endure. That is why St. James said that the "crown of life" is "promised to those who love Him." It is this love that will make you endure to the end and qualify you to receive the crown of life.

1:13 Let no one say when he is tempted, "I am tempted by God"; for God cannot be tempted by evil, nor does He Himself tempt anyone. The word "tempt" here refers to being tempted to commit a sin. Many people when they fall into sins, try to throw the blame on God, as if God had tempted them and enticed them to commit sin. St. James is telling us it is impossible that God tempts us to sin for two reasons: First, God Himself cannot be tempted by sin. Second, God never tempts man to sin. God does not send trials to make us worse, but rather to make us better. How do we fall in sin? St. James answers that in the next verse.

1:14 But each one is tempted when he is drawn away by his own desires and enticed. This is the most beautiful explanation of how sin develops in us. How does temptation grow? It starts with an ungodly desire in your heart. This desire will draw you away from God. At that point you will have left the place of refuge—the place of security; you are drawn away from God. Then, you will be enticed to fall in sin.

In the beginning of the temptation. you are drawn away from God by your own desire. The desire will make you stop going to church, stop reading the Bible, stop praying, stop taking communion, because you want to work with your desire. Such a person allows himself and his own desires and lusts to lead and entice him.

1:15 **Then, when desire has conceived, it gives birth to sin; and sin, when it is full-grown, brings forth death.** We need to look for the root cause of sin: it is in ourselves, not outside of us, because it comes from the inside. Unless you accept sin in your heart, you will never fall into it. Thus, the cause of the sin is usually an ungodly desire in your heart; that is how it starts. Then, when there is an opportunity, you are tempted to fall in sin.

This is reminiscent of the story of Joseph. For him, there was temptation from the outside; his master's wife tried to entice and seduce him. But because his desires were dull, he refused and asked, "How then can I do this great wickedness and sin against God?" (Gen 39:9) There can be no temptation unless something within us causes a sinful desire.

If you sanctify your desires, you will not be tempted; you will be as strong like Joseph. Even if you are surrounded by temptation, you will not be tempted, even the attacks from the devil cannot hurt you unless you make them your own and let them enter inside you.

Satan can attack you from the outside but cannot change your heart unless you give him the key to do so. Sin, therefore, starts from within yourself. Everyone has desires arising from his own foundation, upbringing, temperament, habits, and way of life. The power of Satan lies in his ability to deceive us through enticement. If Satan lost this power, he would be powerless. When he deceives us, he works on our desires to make us believe they are godly. Once we believe our desires are godly and act upon them, we fall into temptation.

when desire has conceived. Desire has conceived when you act upon it — when you add action to it, that will then give birth to sin. Sin is conceived when sinful desire is joined with the will of man. The will plus one's desire will lead to action —to the actual sin.

If I have a desire, such as the love of money, for example, then I start taking money; stealing money, is when sin is conceived. When sinful desire is joined with the will of man (when it is conceived), it will give birth to a sin.

sin, when it is full-grown, brings forth death. When sin grows to maturity, the result is moral and eternal death. It becomes "full-grown" when it is without repentance. When desire is conceived, adding willpower to take action, it will give birth to sin, and sin, when it is full-grown, when you do not repent, brings forth death, both moral and eternal.

1:16 Do not be deceived, my beloved brethren. Do not be deceived about the source of sin. It is not from God. Do not say when you are tempted that God is tempting you. God is the source of all good gifts. The source of sin is your desire.

1:17 Every good gift and every perfect gift is from above, and comes down from the Father of lights, with whom there is no variation or shadow of turning. All gifts are from God. God is the creator of every light of the material world and He is also the source of all the moral lights. "Every good gift and every perfect gift" —good and perfect are from above and come down from the Father of lights. God is the source of the material light, He is also the source of moral light.

with whom there is no variation. God will never give you a bad gift. God will never give you an imperfect gift, because God is unchangeable; He is always the same.

there is no variation or shadow of turning. God is being likened metaphorically to the sun, the source of light. The sun, however, is often causing there to be a shadow, because of the movement of the earth. While the sun is constantly causing various shadows on objects, with God, there is no shadow of turning. He is unchangeable. He is absolute light.

Do not say, "God turned away, so that is why I am living in darkness." If there is such a thing, it is because of us not because of Him. It is not the sun that gives and removes its light, but it is the earth that turns to face the sun's light or turn's away from it, whereby darkness comes.

1:18 Of His own will He brought us forth by the word of truth, that we might be a kind of firstfruits of His creatures. St. James tries to assure us that while you may question your worthiness, God gives good gifts, not because you are worthy, but simply out of His own will. What is His will? His ultimate will is love and purity. That is in stark contrast with our ungodly desires.

He brought us forth as His children by baptism, to those who believed in the "word of truth," the Holy Gospel. When we accept the Gospel, He gives us authority to be the children of God. For those who accept Him and His word, He gives them authority to become children of God, being "brought forth" through baptism.

that we might be a kind of firstfruits of His creatures. The believers will be raised first in the Second Coming of Christ. When St. James says, "we might be a kind of first-fruits of His creatures," he means we are the firstfruits, the first people, who will be risen in the resurrection.

When we think of the meaning of the firstfruits of the Old Testament, believers are the noblest part of the rest of God's creation —sanctifying the rest. Recall how in the Old Testament when the people offered firstfruits. Just by offering the firstfruits, they sanctified the rest. In this way we are the firstfruits. Hence, we are the light of the world and the salt of the earth (Mt 5:13-16), to sanctify the rest of the people.

1:19 **So then, my beloved brethren, let every man be swift to hear, slow to speak, slow to wrath.**

So then. By "so then," St. James signifies a conclusion. He is about to explain a good way to escape temptation. He has already explained that evil comes from our ungodly desires and good gifts come from God; so, how do we escape temptation?

my beloved brethren, let every man be swift to hear, slow to speak, slow to wrath. This is the solution to escaping temptation: Let each one of you hear and listen, hear and learn, be careful not to speak rashly, especially in anger, but be slow to anger, slow to wrath, slow to speak; listen carefully, being "swift to hear" the wisdom of God. This is your protection from temptation.

Many times when we hear something, we get caught up in heated debates and arguments and we end up losing out. We will never get His wisdom this way, not in the manner that will help us overcome temptation, and that is why St. James tells us to be slow to wrath.

You may get heated in debate or be pressed by a feeling of anxiety under some calamity or trial to which the human life is exposed, and as a result, become angry with God. Hastiness of temper hinders hearing the word of God. If you want to avoid temptation, learn from the wisdom of God by listening more, being swift to hear and slow to speak, and do not be quick to anger.

1:20 **for the wrath of man does not produce the righteousness of God.** You will fall into temptation if you get angry, because the wrath of man will not produce the righteousness that you are seeking —the righteousness of God. Some people. in defending God, become very angry. St. James is telling us, "No, this anger cannot produce the righteousness of God."

While you think you are righteous and angrily defending the righteousness of God, actually you are very far from righteousness yourself. In fact, later in Chapter 3, St. James tells us that "righteousness is sown in peace," not in anger. An angry man will show forth something very different from the righteousness of God. (3:18) "The righteousness of God" means all the commandments and all the duties prescribed by God and are pleasing to Him.

that they should grow and flourish.

which is able to save your souls. Poor is the person who does not read the Bible. Poor is the person who does not know the Bible and does not obey it, he is away from salvation. Study the word of God and this will help you attain salvation.

1:21 **Therefore lay aside all filthiness.** The visual that may come to mind is a dirty garment which you take off and lay aside. We should lay aside, as a dirty garment, every impurity of life —all filthiness.

and overflow of wickedness. He speaks here not only of wickedness, but the overflow of it, as if one is consumed by wickedness and has exceeded that even further. What causes the overflowing of wickedness? Wrath and anger.

and receive with meekness. You need to receive the word of God with meekness and modesty rather than with pride. Humble yourself, submit yourself, listen, obey and do the word of God. Receive it into your ears, into your heart, and into your life with meekness.

the implanted word. The "word" is the gospel. It implanted into your heart like seeds implanted with the intention

1:22 **But be doers of the word, and not hearers only, deceiving yourselves.** The word of God will save us when we do as it says. As you are now reading the word of God, after you have finished, if you do not act upon it, the word will not save you. But the word will save you if you are a doer of the word and not only a hearer.

I especially like how St. James phrased it here: be a "doer," not simply "do" the word. "Doer" means all the time, continually carrying out the word of God, as if this becomes your regular business. That is what the Lord said in the conclusion of the Sermon on the Mount: "Therefore whoever hears these sayings of Mine, and does them, I will liken him to a wise man who built his house on the rock." (Mt 7:24)

If you hear the word without doing it, you are deceiving yourself. How? I went to the church, I listened to the Bible, I listened to the gospel, and I heard the word of God; I am righteous.

But no, righteousness does not come just from hearing, but from doing. You are deceiving your own self by thinking that hearing is all that is needed. No, hearing will not save you.

1:23 For if anyone is a hearer of the word and not a doer, he is like a man observing his natural face in a mirror. In the morning, you look at the mirror to see yourself, to see what may need fixing. If you find that something needs adjustment, but instead you do not do anything about it and just leave home, what is the benefit of this mirror? In the same way, the Bible, the word of God, is a mirror. It will show you your weaknesses. It will show you what you need to fix and correct in your life.

If you looked at that mirror and the Bible revealed to you that you have anger, or an unforgiving spirit, or pride, or any other weaknesses, and do nothing to correct what you discover about yourself, what benefit have you received? Thus, while a person may see their natural face in a mirror, the Bible helps the hearer perceive their moral features.

1:24 for he observes himself, goes away, and immediately forgets what kind of man he was. St. James said, "for he observes himself, goes

away"—goes away either to the busy life, to the business of the world, or just to relax his attention after hearing; he let his mind go somewhere else. His interest goes somewhere else. He is not interested in hearing the word of God.

While the Bible helps people observe their moral inadequacies, often they ignore it and simply go away to their busy lives, or the business of the world, or simply relax their attentiveness to what they are hearing. By losing interest in the Bible and shifting your attention elsewhere, you forget all your weaknesses which the Bible can show you. The word of God has potential to leave an impression on you, unless you decide to go away from it, in which case, it will be forgotten.

1:25 But he who looks into the perfect law of liberty. "The perfect law of liberty" is the gospel, because it is the law of freedom. The Lord Jesus Christ set us free; the gospel has set man free.

and continues in it, and is not a forgetful hearer but a doer of the word, this one will be blessed in what he does. Whoever looks into the gospel, the word of God, and allows it to leave an impression on him and obeys the word of God and applies it, will be blessed in whatever he does. Whatever you do will be blessed if you do the word of God.

1:26 If anyone among you thinks he is religious, and does not bridle his tongue but deceives his own heart, this one's religion is useless. Do you want to examine yourself, to see whether or not you are religious? Maybe you go to church and you hear the word of God, and you think that you are religious even though you do not carry out the word of God. If you do not control your tongue, lie, gossip, swear, curse, or judge, you are deceiving yourself because you are not really religious; your religion is useless. The benefit of your religion is to transform you, to change you. If religion does not transform you, it is useless and, also, it is useless in respect of your salvation.

1:27 Pure and undefiled religion before God and the Father is this: to visit orphans and widows in their trouble, and to keep oneself unspotted from the world. After indicating to us what is vain religion (v. 26), St. James tells us two things that constitute "pure and undefiled religion" internal (inward) and external (outward) transformation. Inwardly constitutes whether your heart is unspotted and unstained by sin, then you will have a pure heart. Outwardly, you should help the oppressed and the helpless, such as orphans and widows. Hence, if you find that you have a pure heart inwardly, and outwardly you are eager to help the helpless, then your religion is true.

Pure religion then has these two elements: internal and external. That is what the word of God should produce in you, if you are a doer of the word. If you listen to the word and you do the word of God inwardly, "You are already clean because of the word which I have spoken to you" (Jn 15:3), and outwardly you will find yourself eager to help the helpless.

Chapter 1 Questions

1. What does it mean to be double minded while dealing with God?

2. What is the difference between: "temptation" and "testing of faith"? Think of an example.

3. Explain the different phases we go through while committing sins.

4. What are the steps we should follow when we deal with the word of God so we will be blessed in all that we do?

5. What is "pure and undefiled religion before God"?

2

(in fact, he declares three times that faith without works is dead).

Chapter Outline

Introduction

In this chapter, we will find a call to avoid showing bias or partiality to certain people. St. James gives many reasons for this. Partiality makes a person a judge with evil thoughts (explained further below). Moreover, it is not becoming or befitting behavior for Christians to show partiality. That covers the first half of this chapter (v. 1–13).

In the second half of the chapter, from verses 14 to 26, St. James addresses the relationship between faith and works. He uses a few examples to prove that faith without works is dead, including the example of Abraham, and also the example of Rahab. Note that both of these examples were used by St. Paul as well, when he spoke about faith in the Book of Hebrews, Chapter 11.

We will also look at whether there is any contradiction between St. Paul and St. James, because St. Paul emphasized the importance of faith and St. James spoke about the importance of works

2:1 My brethren, do not hold the faith of our Lord Jesus Christ, the Lord of glory, with partiality. When he used the words "the faith of our Lord Jesus Christ," he was referring to Christianity —the Christian Faith. He is telling us that you cannot be Christian, a believer in the Lord Jesus Christ, and at the same time show partiality.

St. Peter, in his sermon when he visited Cornelius (Acts 10:34) said: "God shows no partiality." If we believe in Christ and we are His children, and are named after Him (being called "Christians"), we should not show partiality. God Himself does not show partiality, whether based on wealth or race or social status.

the Lord of glory. When God does not show partiality, this in itself reflects the glory of God. His glory is apparent in that He does not show partiality. He deals with all equally, whether rich or poor, Gentile or Jew, Barbarian or Greek. Additionally, when we do not show partiality, we are glorifying God.

2:2 **For if there should come into your assembly a man with gold rings, in fine apparel, and there should also come in a poor man in filthy clothes.**

assembly. This means your church; the gathering place for worshiping God together.

a man with gold rings, in fine apparel. Gold rings and fine apparel implies wealth, that this man who has come into church is rich.

and there should also come in a poor man in filthy clothes. The words "filthy clothes" indicate his poverty.

2:3 **and you pay attention to the one wearing the fine clothes and say to him, "You sit here in a good place," and say to the poor man, "You stand there," or, "Sit here at my footstool.** If you show respect to a person because of social status indicating wealth, giving one person honor, a grand welcome, a good seat, while the other you despise and treat scornfully, causing him to stand or to sit in a very uncomfortable place, you are showing partiality. You cannot say, "I am Christian," while you show partiality.

2:4 **have you not shown partiality among yourselves, and become judges with evil thoughts?** If you show partiality based on outward appearances, you are making judgment under the influence of evil thoughts. Maybe you will think to yourself that this rich man will give much money to the church and so you will deal with him in a special way due to the potential of significant contributions, or maybe you will think that this rich man will help your child, give you a job, or will invite you to his inner circle and introduce you to important people who may improve your social status. In all these instances you are making judgments under the influence of evil thoughts.

2:5 **Listen, my beloved brethren: Has God not chosen the poor of this world to be rich in faith and heirs of the kingdom which He promised to those who love Him?** St. James reminds us to think of the poor as the Lord Jesus Christ taught us; He chose His mother St. Mary from among the poor. While we may choose the rich for favors, God has chosen (in most part) the poor to be rich in faith. His mother, the apostles, and those who followed Him were rich in faith in spite of their material poverty, and became heirs of the eternal inheritance rather than contemporary riches.

God does not bestow eternal inheritance based on wealth and social status, but rather gives it to those who love and accept Him.

2:6 But you have dishonored the poor man. Do not the rich oppress you and drag you into the courts? While God exalts the poor man, you often dishonor the poor man. Whom God accepts, you reject. How can you claim you are among His children? St. James was referring to a fact (maybe this fact existed during his time): The oppressors of the poor are usually the rich. How so? Maybe the rich were moneylenders and if the poor did not pay back, they may drag them into courts and bring lawsuits against them to return their debts.

Perhaps he was referring to Christians being persecuted because of their faith, and their persecution was coming from kings, rulers, princes, and other rich individuals. Thus, he asks them that if the rich oppress and drag them into courts, why show partiality and bias in their favor?

2:7 Do they not blaspheme that noble name by which you are called? The noble name by which we are called is the name of Christ, because we are called "Christians." After saying in the previous verse that the rich to whom they have been showing partiality drag them into courts, he points out that they blaspheme the name of Christ.

This blaspheming might come in one of two ways: either rich non-Christians were persecuting Christians and were blaspheming the name of Christ, or maybe they were Christians and because of their bad behavior, oppressing the poor, they were dishonoring the noble name they bear. Here there is an allusion to the fact that maybe the rich were already Christians, but because of their negative behavior of oppressing the poor, they were blaspheming the name of Christ.

2:8 If you really fulfill the royal law according to the Scripture, "You shall love your neighbor as yourself," you do well. The recipients of this letter may object to the claim that they are partial, but they are, in fact, fulfilling the commandment of God to "love your neighbor as yourself." St. James will address this in the next verse saying that to fulfill this royal law of love, it should be done to every person, rich or poor; otherwise, this commandment is not being fulfilled.

2:9 but if you show partiality, you commit sin, and are convicted by the law as transgressors. Partiality transgresses the royal law of loving your neighbor as yourself. Both the rich and the poor alike are our neighbors, but if I am treating the rich in a special way and the poor I dishonor, disrespect, or despise, I am breaking the whole law. That is why it is a sin, disobeying the lawgiver —God.

2:10 **For whoever shall keep the whole law, and yet stumble in one point, he is guilty of all.** "The wages of sin is death" (Rom 6:23). If the law is broken by one commandment, such as the law regarding partiality, the whole law is broken. Breaking the Ten Commandments yields the same punishment as breaking one. He who willfully breaks one commandment is a law-breaker and is guilty of all —guilty of all.

2:11 **For He who said, "Do not commit adultery," also said, "Do not murder." Now if you do not commit adultery, but you do murder, you have become a transgressor of the law.** Sinning against the lawgiver is whether you break one commandment or several. God, who gave one commandment, has also given other commandments. Any sin against God, who gave me the law, makes me a transgressor. Commentary on the next verse clarifies that we are no longer afraid of punishment to the same extent as in the Old Testament.

2:12 **So speak and so do as those who will be judged by the law of liberty.** St. James is saying you should keep the whole law, not out of fear, but rather out of love. Christ now has set you free. The law of liberty is the law of the Gospel, of the New Testament. Now we are not afraid of punishment because God redeemed us on the cross.

When I keep the law, I keep it out of love, because of my freedom in Christ. And yet, as St. Paul said, although Christ has set you free and "you have been called to liberty; only do not use liberty as an opportunity for the flesh." (Gal 5:13) St. James tells us to speak and behave in such a way as ones who, although free, will be judged by the law of liberty.

Do not think that because we are now living in the freedom Christ granted us that there will not be judgment. What is the difference between the law of slavery and the law of liberty? In the law of liberty, I obey the word of God out of love, out of freedom, but in the law of slavery, I am obeying the commandment out of fear. The love of God should cast out fear. The Gospel is not a law seeking outward compulsory actions, but the grace of God gives me a new spirit, regenerating me through baptism, whereby we are born again with a new nature. I do not follow the law out of compulsion and obligation but by my own free will. That is the law of liberty.

2:13 For judgment is without mercy to the one who has shown no mercy. Mercy triumphs over judgment. We will be judged by the law of liberty, but in one of two ways: according to God's justice or according to God's mercy. In the Divine Liturgy, the priest says, "He has appointed a Day for recompense, on which He will appear to judge the world in righteousness, and give each one according to his deeds." The congregation responds, "According to your mercy, O Lord, and not according to our sins."

One of the hymns of the month of Koiahk, "Your mercies O my God," chants unto God: "If you judged us according to your justice, nobody would stand, and so we are appealing to Your mercy." Do you want to be judged by mercy or by justice? If you want to be judged by the mercies of God, you have to show mercy.

Returning to the specific example discussed by St. James, you should show mercy to the poor and not deal with them with partiality. Thus, we must show mercy if we expect mercy. By experiencing and reflecting on God's mercies toward you, your heart will be merciful, and in turn you will show mercy toward others. The mercy that appeared to us in the law of liberty in the gospel is the grace of God. This mercy of God in Christ toward us produces mercy in our hearts toward the poor.

Mercy triumphs over judgment. If we are judged fairly by God, no one will be saved; if, instead, we are judged by God's mercy, we will find salvation. Hence, if we show mercy, we will obtain mercy and triumph over God's judgment. "Blessed are the merciful, for they shall obtain mercy." (Mt 5:7) Although we deserve condemnation, if we deal mercifully with others and refrain from partiality, we will invoke the mercy of God and be judged by that rather than according to what we justly deserve.

In the first half of this chapter, St. James addressed the issue of partiality. In the remaining verses, St. James indicates that if you are a believer, this faith should appear in your behavior (in your "works"). You cannot say, "I am a Christian" while you are showing partiality; show me your Christianity by your behavior. Your faith is dead unless its fruits are works.

2:14 What does it profit, my brethren, if someone says he has faith but does not have works? Can faith save him? Faith without works cannot save. Faith is of no avail unless it demonstrates itself; it must be demonstrated as a living faith by works. If I say I am Christian but my works do not reflect my Christianity, my faith alone will not save me.

2:15–16 **If a brother or sister is naked and destitute of daily food, and one of you says to them, 'Depart in peace, be warmed and filled,' but you do not give them the things which are needed for the body, what does it profit?** St. James gives us practical application of the "royal law" —to "love your neighbor as yourself" (see v. 8 above). Imagine a situation where we are in the church and a brother or a sister comes in naked (i.e., insufficiently clothed—for example, no coat on a cold day, because he is poor, and "destitute of daily food). What if all you did was to only express kind wishes? You would not be showing him mercy here but merely giving nice words: "be warmed, be filled." Such good wishes would be worthless unless followed by active help and practical effort to relieve his suffering.

2:17 **Thus also faith by itself, if it does not have works, is dead.** Just as kind wishes given to a poor and hungry person would not provide him or her much benefit, so too, faith without works is dead. I believe in Christ, but

without practical work, that is nothing —that faith is dead. Faith that has no power to produce works is worthless. Faith cannot stand alone.

2:18 **But someone will say, 'You have faith, and I have works.' Show me your faith without your works, and I will show you my faith by my works.** Faith and works should go hand-in-hand. If you have works but no faith, maybe you are morally acceptable but you lack spirituality, and the works may be hypocrisy because there is no inner faith. Similarly, if you say you have faith but you do not have works, this faith is dead and is merely theoretical. Whether you claim works without faith or faith without works, it is in both cases *nothing*.

2:19 **You believe that there is one God. You do well. Even the demons believe—and tremble!** Even if you know the Christian creed, and you have maintained the right doctrine, even the demons have the same faith, and yet, they will not be saved. No, because they do not have works; they did not repent. If you believe in Christ, your works should reflect your obedience to Christ. Otherwise, your faith alone will not save you. Recall when the Lord Jesus Christ cast out demons, they confessed that he was the "Son of God"

(Mt 8:29), yet that faith was not enough to save them.

2:20 But do you want to know, O foolish man, that faith without works is dead? For the second time, St. James tells us that faith without works is dead, and adds that any other belief is to be deemed foolishness.

2:21 Was not Abraham our father justified by works when he offered Isaac his son on the altar? St. James provides proof for his remarks that faith without works is dead in the example of Abraham. When God asked Abraham to offer his son, Abraham (having previously been told he would be the father of many nations) believed that even if he offered his son and killed him, God would raise him from the dead.

We can see this trust in God in that Abraham told the two servants, "I will go yonder and worship, and we will come back to you" (Gen 22:5). By saying "we" will return, he expresses confidence that both he and Isaac would return after God raises Isaac from death. Similarly, "I will go and worship and we will return to you." He used the plural, "we will return to you." See, he was very, very sure, very confident. St. Paul expresses in his epistle to the Romans that Abraham believed that "God, who gives life to the dead" made alive "the deadness of Sarah's womb" (Romans 4:19).

What if Abraham completely believed that Isaac would be brought back to life again but, nonetheless, did not take Isaac up to be killed and offered to God, would this have been accounted to him for righteousness? It would not, unless Abraham also demonstrated his faith by the work of taking Isaac up the mountain, making the altar, putting Isaac upon it, taking the knife, and raising the knife to offer his son. His faith, in addition to those works, were counted as righteousness, and that is how Abraham was justified.

2:22 Do you see that faith was working together with his works, and by works faith was made perfect? Faith is imperfect without works. As explained regarding the previous verse, Abraham's faith in God without proving his faith with works would have been dead. By works, faith is made perfect.

2:23 And the Scripture was fulfilled which says, 'Abraham believed God, and it was accounted to him for righteousness.' And he was called the friend of God.

In his epistle to the Romans, St. Paul explained that Abraham was the father of the Jews (as his blood descendants) and also of the Gentiles who shared the faith of Abraham (Rom 3). As Abraham was justified by a working faith (demonstrated by his faith when he offered his son, Isaac), so too should all the children of Abraham, both Jew and Gentile, show the working faith of Abraham. Without works, faith is imperfect and dead. Justification and righteousness comes from faith working in love.

And he was called the friend of God. Because of Abraham's working faith, he was honored in such a way that no man was honored, that he received the title "The friend of God."

2:24 **You see then that a man is justified by works, and not by faith only.** Again, St. James repeats the same message, that faith is justified by works. I believe this may be the case because some may have misunderstood the letters of St. Paul (when he spoke about justification by faith). St. Peter wrote regarding St. Paul's letters indicating that many people misinterpret those epistles, twisting them "to their own destruction." (2 Pet 3:15–16) Thus, St. James clarifies as if responding to such people by saying, "No, justification is by works." Hence, faith should work in order to justify you, like the working faith of Abraham.

2:25 **Likewise, was not Rahab the harlot also justified by works when she received the messengers and sent them out another way?** When Joshua sent two messengers to view the land, Rahab expressed her belief that their God is the true God and that He is mighty, recalling how the Lord parted the Red Sea: "The Lord your God, He is God," she said (Josh 2:11). She believed in the God of Israel. The two messengers needed to hide. If she had simply expressed belief in their God as the true God and did nothing else to aid them, would her works profit anyone? Her faith in their God as being the true God turned into actual works by hiding the messengers and sending them out of her house by some other way.

Both St. James and St. Paul (Hebrews 11) cited Abraham and Rahab as examples; St. James uses their example to emphasize the need for faith with works, and St. Paul emphasized their faith. Is there a contradiction between the two?

St. Paul is saying, "If you have all the works but you do not believe in Christ, your works cannot save you." This would be the same answer to the many people who ask about what would happen to a person who is not Christian but does everything right (honest, faithful, does not hurt anyone, etc.). Although he is morally good, if he is not a Christian, St. Paul expresses clearly that works without believing in Christ will not save that person.

On the other hand, St. James is saying, "If you believe in Christ but you do not do the good works to follow, you also will not be saved." Therefore, there is no contradiction. St. Paul is emphasizing the fact that works without believing in Christ is dead, St. James is clarifying that faith, even while believing in Christ, without works, is dead (like the demons who believe in Christ, and yet, are not saved).

2:26 **For as the body without the spirit is dead, so faith without works is dead also.** St. James uses a beautiful metaphor. The body is lifeless without its spirit, in the same way, faith without works is lifeless—dead—and has no power. Works are to faith as spirit is to the body. If you remove works from faith, faith is dead, exactly like when you remove the spirit from the body.

Chapter 2 Questions

1. What is the royal law?

2. What are some examples of partiality mentioned in the epistle?

3. What are the dangers of having partiality between people?

4. Give an example of the dead faith.

5. How did the apostle show the importance of the relationship between faith and work so it can be alive?

6. What is the fate of someone who keeps the whole law but trips in one?

7. Which group of people did St. James mention will be judged with no mercy?

8. How did God deal with poor people?

9. Why did St. James call our Lord Jesus Christ "the Lord of Glory" when he was talking about partiality?

3

Chapter Outline

- The untamable tongue (1-12)
- Heavenly verses demonic (13-18)
- Discussion about the Church (14-16)

Introduction

This chapter addresses two issues which are related to each other: St. James warns us against the desire to become teachers, and on the other hand, if you do become a teacher, then realize you should expect a stricter judgment on Judgment Day.

St. James wants us to be aware of what we should expect on Judgment Day in order to gain sufficient maturity, and also so that we have achieved self-control, especially in controlling our tongues. As a teacher, with your tongue, you explain the oracles of God. Therefore, it is unacceptable that with this same tongue you also curse, or judge, or lie, or commit any other sin.

St. James provides a series of illustrations to teach us about the danger of the tongue (for example, some who desire to be teachers may wish to express, by their tongue, wisdom, simply to appear wise and garner attention for that). That is why St. James later discusses

wisdom, expressing that the wisdom of a person is demonstrated more so by his or her behavior and conduct rather than by their words.

What is the point if I speak wise words but my life does not reflect it? What is the point if I give you wise counseling but my behavior is totally the opposite? St. James compared between earthly and heavenly wisdom—the former causes confusion and every evil thing, while the latter produces the peaceable fruit of righteousness.

3:1 My brethren, let not many of you become teachers, knowing that we shall receive a stricter judgment. When he said, "Let not many of you become teachers," St. James is not speaking of teachers like in schools but rather, he is speaking mainly about teaching in the church—Sunday school servants, priests, etc. Those who teach will be judged more strictly than those who have more humble gifts in the church.

The Lord Jesus Christ told us in the Sermon on the Mount, "With the measure you use, it will be measured back to you." (Mt 7:2) In teaching, we set measures by delineating principles and rules. Therefore, with the same measure it will be measured to me.

Recall also that the Lord said, "For everyone to whom much is given, from him much will be required; and to whom much has been committed, of him they will ask the more." (Lk 12:48) Teachers educate with their tongues, so they will be held accountable more strictly for the manner in which they use their tongue and how they control it.

3:2 For we all stumble in many things. If anyone does not stumble in word, he is a perfect man, able also to bridle the whole body. All of us are liable to stumble and make mistakes. If an ordinary person makes a mistake, maybe people will give him or her an excuse, but when a servant or a teacher makes a mistake, people will hardly excuse them. They will question their teaching, asking, "How come those teachers taught to do so and so, yet, their behavior does not align with what they profess?" Therefore, St. James tells us that the person who controls his tongue gives proof of his ability to maintain entire self-control: "If anyone does not stumble in word, he is a perfect man."

able also to bridle the whole body. We all stumble in many things, but if you can control your tongue, you are a perfect man, able to bridle the whole body. If you control your tongue, this means you have self-control and you can control all other desires. Notice St. James's use of the word "bridle." The word "bridle" brings to mind the figure of a horse and how the bridle bit controls the whole horse, evoking the notion that something that is large can be controlled by something very small.

3:3 Indeed, we put bits in horses' mouths that they may obey us, and we turn their whole body. Through the bridle bit you can control the horse and make him obey you, and control his whole body. Likewise, if you control your tongue, you can control your whole body.

3:4 Look also at ships: although they are so large and are driven by fierce winds, they are turned by a very small rudder wherever the pilot desires. The pilot of a huge ship which is driven by fierce winds, controls the whole ship with a small rudder and helm. This is the same analogy: something small (like the tongue) can control the larger, of which it is but a small part (the whole body).

the pilot desires. Maybe the pilot here refers to our emotions because our emotions dictate what we say with our tongues. If we are angry, maybe we curse; if we are happy, maybe we pray. Thus, the pilot here stands for the emotion. Emotions dictate the tongue, which albeit small, controls the whole body, like the bridle of a horse or like the helm of a ship.

3:5 Even so the tongue is a little member and boasts great things. See how great a forest a little fire kindles! Many times, our tongues claim great power. We give images about ourselves more than who we are. We claim that we achieved great achievements while we did not. This is false boasting and false pride; this little tongue "boasts great things."

See how great a forest a little fire kindles! If you have a very large and great forest, it only takes a little fire to burn it all down. A small spark can burn an entire house. In the same way, this little tongue, with one word, may stir up great trouble and division among people.

3:6 And the tongue is a fire. St. James is referring to the uncontrolled, untamed tongue. One word may cause a war even between countries.

a world of iniquity. The tongue can stir up a world of sinfulness. Satan seduced Eve by words. With the tongue comes a world of sin—we boast, deceive, seduce, and tempt one another

to sin by our tongues.

The tongue is so set among our members that it defiles the whole body. The tongue leads all the body into sin. Temptation, such as seduction, starts with words and ends up with a sexual sin. Words can make the whole body sin in the end.

and sets on fire the course of nature; and it is set on fire by hell. Many wars have started by words. The uncontrolled tongue is inspired by hell, by Satan, and is the organ of the devil.

3:7 For every kind of beast and bird, of reptile and creature of the sea, is tamed and has been tamed by mankind. St. James names four orders: beasts, birds, reptiles, and fish. All of these creatures have been made subject to humans. Although we have succeeded in taming and controlling all these creatures, yet, until now, we struggle in controlling our tongues. Man has never tamed this little organ as a whole.

3:8 But no man can tame the tongue. It is an unruly evil, full of deadly poison. No one can claim that they have never sinned with their tongue. St. James described the tongue as an unruly evil because if it is untamed, it does not follow any rule; the organ itself still does its evil work in the world.

full of deadly poison. The tongue is not only an evil, it is not only unruly, but also, it actually kills and destroys people and nations, contributing to malice, envy, anger, and so forth. That is why he said it is "full of deadly poison."

You can destroy someone with your words, bring them down to such an extent that it is as if you are giving him poison to kill them. Murder is not only physical; you can kill someone emotionally or psychologically.

3:9 With it we bless our God and Father, and with it we curse men, who have been made in the similitude of God. Now St. James illustrates opposing uses for the tongue: we use it to pray and bless God, and sometimes we use our tongues to curse others who are created in the image of God. How can we with the same tongue bless God and curse people who are created in His image? St. James is rebuking some evils he had observed among his people.

3:10 Out of the same mouth proceed blessing and cursing. My brethren, these things ought not to be so. St. James is surprised. How is it that out of the same mouth proceeds both blessing as well as cursing? This inconsistency "ought not to be so." He then appeals to their conscience, signified by calling them "my brethren," and appealing to their brotherhood in Christ, to understand that such conduct deserves the most severe punishment.

Such conduct, when we bless God and curse our brethren, especially from servants and teachers, will receive the most severe punishment. He tells us in the next few verses that even in nature, we do not see such inconsistency.

3:11–12 Does a spring send forth fresh water and bitter from the same opening? Can a fig tree, my brethren, bear olives, or a grapevine bear figs? Thus no spring yields both salt water and fresh. While we humans exhibit inconsistency in the way we use our tongues, in nature we do not see the same thing; for example, we cannot have a well that gives both sweet and bitter water. If even nature does not have this sort of inconsistency, how can we allow the same to be in our lives? We can see a similar feature of a tree, which bears one fruit, not two opposite ones. A fountain of water will not give you both salt and fresh water; likewise, your mouth should not praise God and at the same time be used to curse brethren.

After speaking about teachers and the need to be wary of how the tongue is used, St. James shifts the focus to wisdom. Some people desire to be teachers in order to appear wise to others. He discusses wisdom and compares between heavenly wisdom versus that which is earthly. The main import of his message is that wisdom is shown in conduct and behavior more so than in words. There needs to be consistency with both your words as well as your deeds.

3:13 Who is wise and understanding among you? Let him show by good conduct that his works are done in the meekness of wisdom. If there is a person who is wise and has understanding among you, show your good conduct with humility, which is the most important behavior. If you are prideful and think you are wise, you are, in fact, unwise. Wisdom is demonstrated by meekness and does not speak boastfully or with pride.

3:14 But if you have bitter envy and self-seeking in your hearts, do not boast and lie against the truth. If you believe that you are better than one another and you envy one another with bitterness in your heart, or if you are self-seeking and put your interests before others, you are not showing wisdom. Search your heart. If there is bitterness, envy, or self-seeking there, do not boast of your goodness or wisdom because this will be considered lying against the truth—lying against God, because God is the truth.

3:15 This wisdom does not descend from above, but is earthly, sensual, demonic. "Wisdom" which seeks its own interest and conspires because it envies others, gives rise to envy and strife, division and confusion, so it is not from God. Such wisdom is earthly and worldly, sensual, full of negative passions and emotions. It is from the devil, not from God.

3:16 For where envy and self-seeking exist, confusion and every evil thing are there. With earthly wisdom, there is envy and self-seeking (putting my interest before yours). This all leads to confusion and every evil thing. We will end up divided against each other; all of us will suffer from evil things and confusion will follow.

3:17 But the wisdom that is from

above is first pure, then peaceable, gentle, willing to yield, full of mercy and good fruits, without partiality and without hypocrisy. St. James gives us eight descriptions of heavenly wisdom—"the wisdom that is from above," contrasting it with earthly wisdom. Heavenly wisdom is acquired by communion with God. Earthly wisdom is sensual, but heavenly wisdom is pure. Earthly wisdom is full of strife, but heavenly wisdom seeks peace. Earthly wisdom is stubborn, controlling, and unwilling to yield, but a person with heavenly wisdom is gentle and not too rigid, but rather amenable to persuasion (it is an essential element of heavenly wisdom to be flexible and willing to yield).

Earthly wisdom is not merciful, while heavenly wisdom is full of mercy. Earthly wisdom leads to every evil work and confusion, while heavenly wisdom is full of kindness and good fruits (and the fruit of the Holy Spirit).

Heavenly wisdom is also without partiality, not discriminating among people based on race, religion, gender, or social status. It is also genuinely sincere, without hypocrisy. These are the eight descriptions of heavenly wisdom: pure, peaceable, gentle, willing to yield, full of mercy, full of good fruits, without partiality, and without hypocrisy.

3:18 **Now the fruit of righteousness is sown in peace by those who make peace.** Earthly wisdom causes conflict, division, confusion, and leads to every evil thing. The exact opposite of all of that is peace. The opposite of evil is righteousness. Thus, heavenly wisdom should yield righteousness and the fruit of such righteousness is peace. In order to be righteous, you need to grow in an atmosphere of peace, and this is what heavenly wisdom does.

The farmer who is sowing should also be a peacemaker. Thus, if you are a servant and want your class to be righteous, the fruit of righteousness should be exhibited in peace. The church should have peace and the servant should be the peacemaker. In a home, parents should be peacemakers, and the house should be peaceful with no conflicts, struggle, or fighting, then your children will be righteous.

Peacemakers produce the fruit of righteousness, and peacemakers are those who are truly wise, because heavenly wisdom is peaceable. Those who sow in peace should make sure that the atmosphere of the church, the house, or whatever place, is full of peace.

Chapter 3 Questions

1. Why does St. James caution against many becoming teachers?

2. What is a perfect man?

3. List from verses 6-8 how St. James describes the tongue.

4. Give the example that St. James uses to show how the tongue is often misused in verses 9-10.

5. How does a wise and understanding person reveal himself?

6. What are the characteristics of wisdom that does not descend from above?

7. What exists when there is envy and self-seeking?

8. What are the characteristics of wisdom that is from above?

9. Who produces the fruit of righteousness?

4

Chapter Outline

Introduction

In this Chapter, St. James asks us to consider the source of wars, fighting, and conflict among us. He identifies the problem as being our unsatisfied desires and the love for pleasure which wars within us. The love of pleasures of the world is considered spiritual adultery because we are the bride of Christ. When we fall in love with the world, it is as if we are cheating on Christ, our bridegroom. This, in turn, leads to enmity with God, who yearns for us.

We cannot overcome the love of the world without the grace of God, which is given only to the humble. Hence, if are willing to humble ourselves before God, He will give us grace, and with it, we will be able to overcome the world. That is why St James instructs us to draw near to God in humble submission so that we may receive grace.

Pride is the opposite of humility. Pride can be seen in behavior in various ways, but he spoke about two manners in particular: (1) Judgment (when we speak evil of one another). If I judge my brother, I am arrogant and prideful. Not only that, but I will be a judge of the law, the law of God, instead of being a doer of the law. (2) The other manner that pride is shown is when I plan and boast in my planning without submitting to the will of God. St. James says that we should not make any plans without the will of God, or having the will of God in our minds; otherwise, we are boasting in arrogance.

4:1 Where do wars and fights come from among you? Do they not come from your desires for pleasure that war in your members? At the end of the previous chapter, St. James spoke about peace and explained that the fruit of righteousness is sown in peace by those who make peace. Because he is speaking about peacemakers, he begins to inquire about why the world is full of strife, conflicts, fights, and wars. He identifies the reason as simply: "desires for pleasure"—our desire for the world and its vanity.

among you. St. James was the bishop of Jerusalem. In this letter, he is not only addressing Christians, but also Jews who did not yet convert to

Christianity. He still cares about his brethren (according to the flesh) and is addressing them to see why they fight and war with one another.

He sounds like one of the prophets of the Old Testament, like the Prophet Jeremiah or the Prophet Amos, when they were rebuking the people. He tells them that the reason behind wars and conflicts is due to their pursuit of pleasures which are not satisfied, and which will lead to sin.

4:2 **You lust and do not have. You murder and covet and cannot obtain. You fight and war. Yet you do not have because you do not ask.** Continuing his remarks from the previous verse, he explains what happens when people desire something but do not obtain what they seek.

You murder. You will kill, and maybe afterward will take the person's belongings so that you will have what you desire from that person.

and covet and cannot obtain. Although you wanted to satisfy your desires by killing and coveting, you cannot obtain enough to satiate yourself. This reminds me of King Ahab in the Old Testament, when he desired to take the field of Naboth the Jezreelite and so he killed him, yet he was not able to obtain peace in his heart. (1 Kg 21) Elijah the Prophet rebuked him by

relaying God's message: "In the place where dogs licked the blood of Naboth, dogs shall lick your blood, even yours." (1 Kg 21:19) Sins like murder, hatred, envy, and covetousness are the result of unsatisfied desires.

Notice that hatred and the covetousness are precursors to murder. A person does not go and just kill someone (usually), but it starts from within the heart, with hatred or covetousness, and the like. For King Ahab, it began with covetousness and the envy of Naboth, which led to murdering him.

You fight and war. Yet you do not have because you do not ask. When you do not obtain what you seek you will begin fighting and warring with one another in order to satisfy your greed and, yet, you will find that you are still unsatisfied.

In order to satisfy one's desires, a person must ask God. He is the provider and will satisfy all our needs, whether they are physical, spiritual, emotional, social, or psychological—*all* our needs.

Maybe God will not give us what we ask for, but he will give us contentment. That is why we will feel satisfied. That is why St. James told them they should humbly go to God with their requests. Lusting, fighting, envying, hating, coveting, and killing will not satisfy your desires.

4:3 You ask and do not receive, because you ask amiss, that you may spend it on your pleasures. Many wonder why they ask to receive satisfaction from God but do not seem content. Be certain that if you are not asking according to God's will (for example, seeking that God conceal your thefts, or help you kill someone), God will not answer your prayers. That is why St. James says, "You ask and do not receive, because you ask amiss, that you may spend it on your pleasures."

Some people pray to satisfy their lusts, but God does not answer such prayers. I remember one time I was reading some of the small papers left on the altar, and I found one apparently written by a teenage girl. She wrote in her prayer, "God, please let Dad and Mom accept my boyfriend." She is praying, but do you think God will answer her prayer? "Seek first the kingdom of God and His righteousness, and all these things shall be added to you." (Mt 6:33)

4:4 Adulterers and adulteresses! Do you not know that friendship with the world is enmity with God? Whoever therefore wants to be a friend of the world makes himself an enemy of God. He speaks here about spiritual adultery. We are spouses of Christ, the bride of Christ. When we love the world, it is as if we are committing fornication with the world, cheating on our bridegroom.

Do you not know that friendship with the world is enmity with God? I cannot befriend God and the world at the same time because the prince of this world is Satan and, therefore, a friend of this world is opposed to Christ.

The spirit that is working in the world is the spirit of Satan, which is also in opposition to Christ. If I love the world with its pleasures and lusts, I am in enmity with God. You cannot love God and the world at the same time, as the Lord taught us: "No one can serve two masters; for either he will hate the one and love the other, or else he will be loyal to the one and despise the other. You cannot serve God and mammon." (Mt 6:24)

Whoever therefore wants to be a friend of the world makes himself an enemy of God. It is your decision, it is your choice: either to be the bride of Christ or to be the friend of the world. If you choose to be a friend of the world and to satisfy your pleasures from the world and to seek its vanity, you will become an enemy to God.

In every Divine Liturgy, after the Catholic Epistle is read, the Church reminds us, "Do not love the world or the things in the world. The world shall pass away and all its pleasures, but those who do the will of God will abide forever." (1 Jn 2:17)

4:5 **Or do you think that the Scripture says in vain, 'The Spirit who dwells in us yearns jealously?'** This verse confuses many people. Which Spirit and what Scripture are being referred to here? St. James is quoting from the Book of Deuteronomy 32:1–47. In this passage, we can see God's love and jealousy for His people, as a groom jealous for his bride, or as a husband jealous for his wife. God is also jealous for us. So, the "Spirit" here refers to the Holy Spirit, whom we received in the Holy Mystery of Confirmation after Baptism, who desires us jealously.

He wants to be with us; He wants to unite us with God, but God desires that we should not commit adultery with the world (i.e., fall in love with the world); this will make Him jealous. He wants us to be wholly devoted to Him because we are espoused to Him; we are His bride, His wife.

I can even say that God envies the world when the world attracts our love and attracts our attention. God loves you very much, so do not provoke His jealousy when you befriend the world. You may tell me, "It is difficult to overcome the love of pleasures and resist the love of the world." St. James gives us an answer to this dilemma in the next verse.

4:6 **But He gives more grace. Therefore He says: 'God resists the proud, But gives grace to the humble.'**

But He gives more grace. God is willing to give us His grace to enable us to overcome our love for the world. Just ask for His grace and He will give it to you, and you will be able to overcome the love of the world because you will be satisfied and will say with David, "And there is none upon earth that I desire besides You." (Ps 73:25)

God resists the proud, but gives grace to the humble. The grace of God is obtained through humility (cf. Proverbs 3:34). You need to humble yourself, submit yourself to God, then grace will come to you. By His grace, you will overcome the world and all its desires.

St. James sends a message in the next four verses (7–10): humility will cure our love for the world.

4:7 **Therefore submit to God. Resist the devil and he will flee from you.** Submit yourself to God to secure His grace. There are practical ways to submit:

Resist the devil and he will flee from you. Satan always flees before solid resistance, as we saw in the temptation of Christ on the mountain when Christ resisted the devil, the devil left him. Resist the devil and the devil will flee. If you do not push the devil back, if you do not resist him, the devil will press more into your territory. He wants to take more space in your life, but if you resist him, he will leave you alone—he will flee and escape.

4:8 **Draw near to God and He will draw near to you. Cleanse your hands, you sinners; and purify your hearts, you double-minded.** If you wish that God is near and close to you, you must seek to dwell very near to Him. This can be accomplished by prayer, worship, studying and memorizing His words, fasting, and through the Mysteries of Repentance and Confession and the Holy Eucharist.

Draw near to Him through fasting and prayer. All these practices will help you draw near to God and submit to Him. Then, God will give you His grace by which you will be able to overcome the love of the world.

Cleanse your hands, you sinners. Besides resisting the devil, submitting to God means repenting. "Cleanse your hands" does not refer to the literal washing of your hands but, rather, it refers to purifying of your actions, words, and deeds. Your deeds should be according to God's will, because sin keeps you away from Him.

and purify your hearts, you double-minded. He speaks here about the heart and the mind, and how we can reconcile our hearts and our minds in this world. You cannot submit to God in double-mindedness, where you heart seeks both God and the world. This is reminiscent of Elijah when he warned the people, "If the Lord is God, follow Him; but if Baal, follow him" (1 Kg 18:21).

You cannot have a divided heart because that would mean it is impure. You need to purify your heart from the love of the world by devoting your heart in complete dedication to God. In this way, you will not be double-minded.

4:9 **Lament and mourn and weep!** Develop godly sorrow. St. Paul speaks about such sorrow at length in 2 Corinthians, Chapter 7, where he explains that "godly sorrow produces repentance leading to salvation, not to be regretted" (2 Cor 7:10). Instead of enjoying the pleasures of the world, develop godly sorrow and repent.

Let your laughter be turned to mourning and your joy to gloom. Here, "joy" means the joy of the world; the fun of the world that is not according to the will of God, which is totally different from the joy which is the fruit of the Holy Spirit. Instead of trying to satisfy your desires through ungodly entertainment and ungodly fun, let your laughter be turned into mourning, repentance, and godly sorrow; mourn over your sins, and sincerely repent of them.

4:10 Humble yourselves in the sight of the Lord, and He will lift you up. The key to overcoming the love of the world is to humble yourself and submit to God, and He will give you the grace by which you will be lifted up above the world and set free from being attached to it.

in the sight of the Lord. This refers to continually feeling God's presence. As you humble yourself, you will know you are in the presence of God. A tree, in order to grow upward, must dig its roots deep below the ground. In the same way, in order for you to be exalted, in order for you to be lifted up above the world, you must be deeply rooted by humility and submission into His pure mind.

He will lift you up in this world, and eventually you will be lifted up out of it to come into eternal life. St. Augustine said: "As I became a youth, I longed to be satisfied with worldly things, and I dared to grow wild in a succession of various and shadowy loves…." Yet, he overcame the world, he says, when he no longer desired anything from it; he became content. God satisfied and fulfilled all his desires and all his pleasures.

4:11 Do not speak evil of one another, brethren. He who speaks evil of a brother and judges his brother, speaks evil of the law and judges the law. Speaking evil means to harshly judge others. When I judge my brother, I am violating the "royal law," which is to "love your neighbor as yourself" (Jam 2:8). Since the royal law requires loving our brother, this law is violated when harshly judging others. It is as if we are condemning the law itself, speaking ill of it, regarding it as a commandment that is not worth following or is not good enough.

By your actions, you are expressing that this law is not one by which you can live. Many people say that this commandment does not fit today; thus, we are judging the law.

But if you judge the law, you are not a doer of the law but a judge. God gives us commandments, It is not for us to say whether these commandments are good or bad. Our sole objective is to fulfill His commandments, not question them. It is not your place to judge God's commandments (e.g., saying that this law is applicable to modern times, and that law is no longer applicable). When you sit as a judge, you are no longer a humble and faithful doer of the commandment of God; you will have lost your humility. Do not expect God to give you His grace if you judge His laws.

4:12 There is one Lawgiver, who is able to save and to destroy. Who are you to judge another? The Lawgiver is God, the Almighty and the Judge. God is the only one who can save and destroy, who can punish and reward; it is not your place. When you judge your brother, you are arrogant, placing yourself in the place of God, misappropriating His authority. After this, do you expect to receive grace from God? His grace is given to the humble, not to the proud.

4:13 Come now, you who say, 'Today or tomorrow we will go to such and such a city, spend a year there, buy and sell, and make a profit;' Another sign of pride is when you boast about the future. You speak in arrogance: "I will do this, I will do this, I will do that," as if you are confident it will happen. Recall the parable involving the foolish rich man who said he would destroy the storage buildings he built to build larger ones to store even more food so that he could eat and enjoy for many years to come. God called him foolish and said that night his soul would be taken from him.

Can you really be certain about what will happen in the future? Can you even guarantee your life until tomorrow morning? St. James is exposing to us the foolishness of making plans about the future without submitting to God's will. I do not want anybody to misunderstand. I am not saying do not make plans for the future, but when you are making these plans, keep the will of God in your mind, considering that maybe you will meet God now. You should always say, "If it is according to God's will, I will do so and so," as St. James taught us here.

4:14 whereas you do not know what will happen tomorrow. For what is your life? It is even a vapor that appears for a little time and then vanishes away. How can you confidently make plans about tomorrow while you do not know anything about the future or whether you will even have tomorrow morning? Our life is like a vanishing vapor, beginning in appearance to be very thick, but in a few moments, vanishes away, disappearing completely. That is life.

How many people have we heard about who suddenly departed from this world? They were living with us, then suddenly they were not here; it is as if they disappeared. So, too, our lives are like a vanishing vapor. We should not place our confidence in life, but in God.

4:15–16 Instead you ought to say, 'If the Lord wills, we shall live and do this or that.' But now

you boast in your arrogance. All such boasting is evil. The proper way to proceed with life and planning for the future is to submit everything to God's will and say, "If it is God's will, we will do this or that." But this is not just a word. Many of us are accustomed to saying, "God willing." It is more an attitude than just words. When, however, you plan for the future without keeping God's will in your mind, you are exuding arrogance rather than humility. All such boasting is evil before God, and you cannot receive His grace to overcome the world and its desires in such a manner.

4:17 Therefore, to him who knows to do good and does not do it, to him it is sin. In other words, St. James is saying, "Now that I have taught you how to overcome the world, and how you should be good and humble yourself to receive God's grace, you have to do right as I taught you." If we do not do what is right and, yet, we knew what we should do, the sin is greater upon us because of our knowledge.

Chapter 4 Questions

1. To whom is St. James addressing the following question in verse 1: "Where do wars and fights come from among you?"

2. Where do wars and fights find their origin?

3. What does the phrase "you ask and do not receive" mean?

4. What does the phrase "friend of the world" mean and how can that cause an enmity with God?

5. What counsel does St. James give to those tempted by the world?

6. Why should we be careful about the plans we make?

5

Chapter Outline

- Rich oppressors will be judged (1-6)
- Be patient and persevere (7-12)
- Meeting specific needs (13-18)
- Bring back the erring one (19-20)

Introduction

This is the last chapter in this epistle and it begins with a strong condemnation against the rich who oppress the poor. St. James was most likely speaking about rich non-believers. After this, he focuses on the poor and asks them to patiently wait for the coming of the Lord, He will save them when He comes. Holding onto patience, he warned them not to grumble against one another.

St. James concludes this chapter by giving some practical instructions. He tells the recipients of this letter to pray if they are suffering and praise if they are rejoicing. He also tells them if they are sick to call the priest of the church to perform the Mystery of the Unction of the Sick and anoint them with oil if they are ill, assuring them that God will answer the prayers of the faithful and will raise the sick persons, and forgive theirs sins if they confess and take personal responsibility. He tells people

that the fervent prayers of a righteous man avails much, recalling the story of Elijah and how by his prayers the heavens closed and opened.

In the final verse, he tells us that by turning a sinner from error, you are saving a soul from death, because the wages of sin is death.

5:1 Come now, you rich, weep and howl for your miseries that are coming upon you! The expression, "come now," is the same expression he used in James 4:13. There, he was rebuking those who desired riches; here, in this chapter, however, he is rebuking those who use riches wickedly. He was not confining his remarks merely to the people living in his days, but he is speaking to people for all ages in all generations.

He tells them to weep and lament because the judgment of their sins is coming upon them soon. Maybe he was referring to the rich in Jerusalem (as he was the bishop of Jerusalem who suffered a lot during the fall of Jerusalem and the destruction of the temple). He wanted them to recognize that living in righteousness will save them, unlike their riches, which will not save them on the difficult Day of the Coming of the Lord, who will come and give to each one according to his deeds, whether good or evil.

5:2 Your riches are corrupted, and your garments are moth-eaten. Aside from the readily apparent meaning of this verse, that the riches in which they trusted had been corrupted or spoiled, this verse has another meaning. He wants to tell them, "Instead of using this money to help the poor and the needy, you stored this money, to the extent that it rusted and moths ate your garments."

During the time in which this epistle was written, people used to store their wealth in various manners of storage. However, because of improper care, much of this wealth often became corrupted or spoiled. Thus, he is referring to garments, which instead of distributing them to the poor, were stored and never used, and were ruined. Also, the riches that were stored were never used as they should have been.

5:3 Your gold and silver are corroded, and their corrosion will be a witness against you and will eat your flesh like fire. If you think about gold and silver, they do not really rust, so what is meant by "corrosion" here is that they actually changed in color. The

message he is trying to convey is that these items were stored without any use, instead of utilizing them to help others in need. Thus, these items will stand against the rich as witnesses of their stinginess and lack of generosity in not helping the poor.

Thus, these same items will punish you "and will eat your flesh like fire," because you will suffer from the Judgment of the Lord, because you did not help the poor and needy. This will expose you to the fire of hell.

You have heaped up treasure in the last days. Usually, when we think about the Second Coming of Christ or about the end of life, we do not think about our need to store but rather our need to distribute (to the poor, for example), in order to gain treasure in heaven; not to store things that should be given away.

We should not lay up treasures here, but lay up treasures in heaven, as the Scripture teaches us, "Do not lay up for yourselves treasures on earth, where moth and rust destroy and where thieves break in and steal; but lay up for yourselves treasures in heaven, where neither moth nor rust destroys and where thieves do not break in and steal. For where your treasure is, there your heart will be also" (Mt 6:19–21).

Stored, undistributed wealth, will curse the owner. Instead of laying up treasure in heaven, you will have continued to pile up earthly treasures. Instead of directing your money to benefit you at the coming of the Lord at the Last Day, you actually stored this money. This is extreme foolishness. Recall the parable of the foolish rich man who continued to store more and more until God one day told him that he was foolish and that he would die that day, and what he had stored would not go with him. (Lk 12)

in the last days. This may refer either to the coming of the Lord or instead to the destruction of Jerusalem, which occurred in AD 70 during the reign of Emperor Titus.

5:5 **You have lived on the earth in pleasure and luxury; you have fattened your hearts as in a day of slaughter.** Instead of being generous and fair and just, the rich are being criticized for using their wealth and spending their money on their own pleasures and luxurious living. St. James recalls animals who are fed and made fat only in the end to be killed (to be eaten). Similarly, the rich fatten their hearts as in the day of slaughter, feasting and engaging in pleasures without paying attention to the day of slaughter—the Day of the Lord—which is coming soon. All this pleasure would soon be turned to judgment.

5:4 **Indeed the wages of the laborers who mowed your fields, which you kept back by fraud, cry out; and the cries of the reapers have reached the ears of the Lord of Sabaoth.** St. James rebukes the rich for oppressing laborers, deceiving them by fraud, and not giving them their wages, all of which causes them to cry to God because of their oppression. Their cry has reached God's ears, just as God heard the cries of Israel when they were oppressed by the hand of Egypt. This act of keeping back the pay owed to laborers is denounced several times in the Bible: Leviticus 19:13, Deuteronomy 24:14, Jeremiah 22:13, Malachi 3:5, and Job 24:6.

5:6 **You have condemned, you have murdered the just; he does not resist you.** This verse is applicable to laborers (see verse 4 above), but it can also refer to the Lord Jesus Christ, "the just" who was "murdered." As mentioned previously, James was the bishop of Jerusalem and is speaking to Jewish people, telling them they have condemned and murdered the just one—the Lord Jesus Christ.

They crucified Him, which brought upon them condemnation and destruction. It was the rich and influential, not the poor, who sought His death. And He did not resist, as it was written about Christ by the Prophet Isaiah: "He was oppressed and He was afflicted, yet He opened not His mouth; He was led as a lamb to the slaughter, and as a sheep before its shearers is silent, so He opened not His mouth" (Isaiah 53:7).

From verses 1 to 6, St. James spoke about how the rich oppressors will be judged. From verses 7 to 12 he speaks about how to be patient and persevering.

5:7 Therefore be patient, brethren, until the coming of the Lord. See how the farmer waits for the precious fruit of the earth, waiting patiently for it until it receives the early and latter rain. After he finished talking to the Jews who were rich and not following God's commandments, St. James addressed his suffering and oppressed brethren, asking them to be patient because the Lord would come soon and will bring them relief from persecution. He gave them three examples of patience:

See how the farmer waits for the precious fruit of the earth, waiting patiently for it. The farmer has to sow and plant seeds, and after this, he will wait a long time with patience for fruit to appear. St. James encourages his oppressed brethren to patiently wait for the Lord like the farmer who waits for his crop.

until it receives the early and latter rain. The early rain is the shower, which prepares the ground to receive seeds. The latter rains are the showers needed to bring the harvest to maturity. As the farmer waits patiently for the early and latter rains to come so that his seeds mature and produce fruit, so too, says St. James, should his oppressed brethren patiently wait for the coming of the Lord.

5:8 You also be patient. Establish your hearts, for the coming of the Lord is at hand. This, he reiterates what was expressed in the previous verse.

5:9 Do not grumble against one another, brethren, lest you be condemned. Behold, the Judge is standing at the door! Some people when they are oppressed, their attitude is to complain and grumble against others. St. James reminds them that as Christians they should not judge others, for only God is the Judge. Instead, wait patiently rather than bear grudges in your hearts against one another; otherwise you will be condemned, because if you judge, you will be judged, because you have taken the place of God.

Let the Lord judge the oppressors, not you. The Lord is the One who will condemn them, not you. His coming is at hand, so wait patiently, do not judge one another, do not grumble against one another, and do not complain against one another.

similar end as Job.

and seen the end intended by the Lord – that the Lord is very compassionate and merciful. Job, having received blessings from God as a reward for patiently enduring, did not happen by chance, but was in fact "intended by the lord;" this was God's plan for Job out of God's economy.

Job persevered patiently, so God gave him double of everything he lost. This blessing that came upon Job demonstrates that the Lord is full of compassion and He is merciful.

5:10 **My brethren, take the prophets, who spoke in the name of the Lord, as an example of suffering and patience.** After giving the example of the farmer in verse 8, the second example of patience is in the example of the prophets who suffered patiently and endured to the end, so they were blessed. These prophets, whose main mission was to deliver messages from God to the people ("who spoke in the name of the Lord"), suffered for what they had to say; yet, they diligently waited patiently for God.

5:11 **Indeed we count them blessed who endure. You have heard of the perseverance of Job and seen the end intended by the Lord—that the Lord is very compassionate and merciful.** We believe that those who endure will have a final reward; they will be blessed.

You have heard of the perseverance of Job. St. James gives his third and final example of patience in the enduring patience of Job. He refused to distrust God in spite of all odds against him, and in the end, God blessed him and doubled everything he had. St. James is trying to encourage the oppressed, indicating that they too will receive a

5:12 **But above all, my brethren, do not swear, either by heaven or by earth or with any other oath. But let your 'Yes' be 'Yes,' and your 'No,' 'No,' lest you fall into judgment.** St. James is telling them, "I do not have to swear to you to make you believe that if you wait patiently God will bless you; you should take my 'Yes' as 'Yes,' and my 'No' as 'No.' I have given you three examples (the farmer, the prophets, and Job) to show you how God rewards and blesses perseverance and patience."

Some people swear by using the name of the Lord in vain. St. James makes clear we should not do this—neither by swearing by heaven or earth nor taking any other such oath. In fact, he is quoting the words of the Lord Jesus Christ in the Sermon on the Mount in Matthew 5:33-37. Unfortunately, swearing is a common sin until this day.

Be honest. If you are asked to do something, be frank about whether you will or will not keep your commitment. Verse 12 can also be taken to mean either that we should be honest and not lie, or it can mean that if you say something, you should keep your word and follow through with it. If you cannot, just be clear up front. Do not say you will do something and not do it.

Whenever you make a commitment, take care to ensure you make it happen. Some people say they have trouble saying "No," so they will say they will try to do something but do not complete what they said they would do. You, however, as a Christian, should let your "Yes" be "Yes" and "No" "No"; or otherwise, you will fall into judgment. Those who swear, lie, and are dishonest, will be judged.

From verses 13 to 15, St. James is addressing specific needs.

5:13 **Is anyone among you suffering? Let him pray. Is anyone cheerful? Let him sing psalms.** If someone is suffering, instead of blaming God or others, improperly using your tongue by cursing and judging. If you suffer or are afflicted, do not engage yourself in any improper use of the tongue; rather, you need to pray. God

is your helper in such moments of difficulty.

Is anyone cheerful? Let him sing psalms. If you are cheerful, do not rejoice as do the children of the world, conforming yourself and imitating their ways of expressing joy in ungodly ways. Instead, express your joy by praising the Lord through singing psalms. Let your joy be shown not only in speech but also in singing psalms, giving thanks to God and praising Him. Prayer and thanksgiving are the appropriate expressions when one is suffering or is cheerful.

5:14 **Is anyone among you sick? Let him call for the elders of the church, and let them pray over him, anointing him with oil in the name of the Lord.** Here, we find reference to the Mystery of the Unction of the Sick. If you are sick, St. James advises you to call the "elders," that is, the priests. [Note: The word "elders" is used in the Protestant texts of the Holy Scripture because the Priesthood is not an observed sacrament in this denomination. However, the Orthodox and Catholic Churches use the term "priests," as in presbyter, because the Holy Mystery of the Priesthood is observed.]

Let them pray over him, anointing him with oil in the name of the Lord. In the Mystery of the Unction of the Sick, the infirm will be anointed with oil, which is a channel for the Holy Spirit to give healing to the person. The priest also lays hands over the sick person, and the Holy Spirit heals the ailing person.

This oil does not refer merely to medicine, but rather an actual Mystery. Because Protestants do not believe in the Mystery of the Unction of the Sick, they question what the oil is referring to in this passage, presuming it to refer to medicine as was used during that time.

If you remember the parable of the good Samaritan (Lk 10:25-37), oil and wine were used to help the person in need; thus, Protestants deny this Mystery. However, this is wrong. This passage specifically says that the oil is to be placed "in the name of the Lord," which signifies that this is a Mystery. Recall that Christ asked the apostles to anoint the sick with oil, too, in Luke Chapter 10, which further attests to the fact that this is a priestly function.

5:15 **And the prayer of faith will save the sick, and the Lord will raise him up. And if he has committed sins, he will be forgiven.** Prayer for the sick must be offered in faith in order to be effective. Recall that the Lord Jesus Christ, before performing any miracle used to ask, "Do you believe?" So, when you pray for the

sick, pray with faith for your prayer to be effective. When you pray with faith, this prayer will save the sick and the Lord will raise him up.

This does not mean literal healing, because St. Paul prayed with faith three times to be healed from a thorn in the flesh, but God did not heal him (cf. 2 Cor 12:7–10). Rather, this means that God will do what is best for this person. God chose to keep the thorn of the flesh in St. Paul to keep him humble, and this was deemed as best for St. Paul.

And if he has committed sins, he will be forgiven. Sometimes, our diseases are because of our sins. I say sometimes because not every disease is caused by sin, but there are some diseases that can be attributed to sin. For example, smoking can lead to cancer in the lungs, drinking alcohol can lead to liver failure, drugs can lead to destruction of cells in the brain, sexual immorality can lead to sexually transmitted diseases, and partaking of the Eucharist in an unworthy manner can lead to some physical diseases, as St. Paul said in 1 Corinthians 11.

Therefore, if your disease is because of your sins, you need to repent and to confess. If you confess your sins, as St. James said, you "will be forgiven." The Lord, who raised the sick in answer to prayer, will also forgive our sins when we repent and confess (as indicated in the next verse).

5:16 Confess your trespasses to one another, and pray for one another, that you may be healed. The effective, fervent prayer of a righteous man avails much. This verse serves as another Scriptural reference to the Mystery of Confession. Protestants proclaim that if you sin against someone, just go and tell him, "I am sorry." However, St. John Chrysostom and St. Augustine both reject that understanding.

When I tell you, "treat one another," I mean the physician should treat the sick. When I tell you "teach one another," I mean the teacher should teach the student. Thus, when St. James said, "Confess your trespasses to one another," he meant the priest and clergy should receive the confession of the repentant.

and pray for one another, that you may be healed. Healing will be made evident in both body and spirit. We all need healing of our sins. Thus, healing is not only physical, but spiritual healing also—healing of our bodies, and our souls, and our spirits.

Confessing your sins is evidence of your repentance because when you confess your sins, you acknowledge your transgressions; you take responsibility for your trespasses, and you ask the priest to hold you accountable. In addition to repentance and confession, prayer is also conditional for the forgiveness of sin.

The effective, fervent prayer of a righteous man avails much. In order for your prayer to be effective, you need to offer your prayer with faith and zeal, so that it is offered fervently, and you must be righteous, which means you are living the life of repentance. "The effective, fervent prayer of a righteous man avails much." This means that such prayer will do things beyond our expectations. For proof, St. James tells us of the story of Elijah in the next verse (cf. 1 Kg 17).

5:17 Elijah was a man with a nature like ours, and he prayed earnestly that it would not rain; and it did not rain on the land for three years and six months. Elijah was a simple human, not supernatural. He was a man like all other men but achieved great results because of his prayers, due to their being offered with faith and zeal, and because he was righteous.

and he prayed earnestly that it would not rain; and it did not rain on the land for three years and six months. Through Elijah's prayers, he was able to close heaven and open it again, to stop the rain and to bring it again. Take note here that the exact timeframe of "three years and six months" was not stated in the Old Testament but, rather, St. James writes what he learned from Tradition, and also by the inspiration of the Holy

Spirit. St. James wrote the exact time based on the Holy Tradition, and by the inspiration of the Holy Spirit.

5:18 And he prayed again, and the heaven gave rain, and the earth produced its fruit. We find this second prayer, when Elijah "prayed again," in 1 Kings 18:42. His prayer was offered on Mount Carmel after Elijah killed all the priests of Baal. Afterward, God sent rain on the earth and it produced its fruit.

5:19 Brethren, if anyone among you wanders from the truth, and someone turns him back. This can either refer to a false belief system or false doctrine, or it can refer to some false practice.

5:20 let him know that he who turns a sinner from the error of his way will save a soul from death and cover a multitude of sins. This should encourage all of us to work to serve in restoring fallen brethren, seeking out the lost sheep and bringing them back to the fold, looking for the prodigal son and having him return. St. James wants us to notice that we are participating in a great work because we are saving a

soul from death. This is not physical death but an eternal death, because "the wages of sin is death" (Rom 6:23).

and cover a multitude of sins. When you bring someone back to Christ, not only do you save him from eternal death, you also cover his sins. The word "cover" is used here because the blood of Jesus Christ has covered our sins so that we may be forgiven. This is the only way for our sins to be forgiven. "Cover" here also means you will restore the person back without exposing him for what he has done; instead, you will keep whatever he did as a secret and maintain confidentiality.

Chapter 5 Questions

1. "Therefore, because you tread down the poor and take grain taxes from him, though you have built houses of hewn stone, yet you shall not dwell in them; you have planted pleasant vineyards, but you shall not drink wine from them .For I know your manifold transgressions and your mighty sins: Afflicting the just [and] taking bribes; diverting the poor [from justice] at the gate" (Amos 5:11-12). Which verses from James 5 is giving the same meaning as these verses from Amos?

2. Is it wrong to live in pleasure and luxury?

3. "Be glad then, you children of Zion, and rejoice in the LORD your God; for He has given you the former rain faithfully, and He will cause the rain to come down for you—The former rain, and the latter rain in the first [month]" (Joel 2:23). What is the difference between irrigation from rivers or from rains? And what is the spiritual meaning to us?

4. "He shall come down like rain upon the grass before mowing, like showers [that] water the earth" (Psalm 72:6). The rain falling refers to what?

5. Why does God condemn us when we grumble against one another?

6. In James 5:13-15, St. James gave us practical solutions for many different cases in our lives. Discuss these solutions and cases.

7. St. James mentioned two of the Church Mysteries in this chapter; what are they?

8. Is there a relationship between healing the sickness and confession?

9. "The effective, fervent prayer of a righteous man avails much." What proof from this chapter supports this statement?

10. What is the Honor of one who saves (turn back) a sinner?

The First Epistle of

Peter

AUTHOR: St. Peter. The author, as indicated in 1:1, is St. Peter. He was one of the twelve disciples whom the Lord Jesus called along with his brother Andrew. St. Peter described himself in Chapter 5 as "a witness of the sufferings of Christ," because he was His disciple and actually followed Him to the cross. After the resurrection of the Lord, they [the disciples and apostles] spent forty days with Him until His ascension. The first homily, which was given on the Day of Pentecost, was given by St. Peter. Thus, he described himself as a "witness of the sufferings of Christ." Also, the early Church Fathers confirmed that the author of this letter is St. Peter, namely: Irenaeus AD 185; St. Clement of Alexandria, AD 200; Tertullian, AD 200; and Eusebius, AD 300. Silvanus, who is also Silas, assisted St. Peter in writing this letter. Silas and Paul journeyed together on the second missionary trip, but in Chapter 5:12 St. Peter mentions Silvanus, who is also Silas,

as the co-writer of this letter. Silas, as we read in the Book of Acts, was a well-known prophet and a missionary in the early Church. Silas joined St. Paul in writing some of his letters, like First Thessalonians and Second Thessalonians, where St. Paul mentions Silas in the introduction. Therefore, Silas participated in writing three letters: two with St. Paul and one with St. Peter.

PLACE & TIME: We know that St. Peter and St. Paul were martyred during the reign of Nero, and we know from history that Nero committed suicide in the year AD 68. That is why this letter must be dated before AD 68. Some Church Fathers say that this letter was written on the eve of the Neronian persecution, which was around AD 63-64. In Chapter 4, St. Peter spoke about "the fiery trial that is now happening," which is a reference to the persecution that was started by Nero, when St. Peter told them, "Do not consider it a strange thing when you look at the fiery trial that is now happening."

In Chapter 5:13, St. Peter indicates that he wrote this letter from "Babylon," but which Babylon? Is it Babylon, Iraq, or did he use this word as a code for Rome or Jerusalem? Papias (AD 125), who was one of the Apostolic Fathers , as well as Irenaeus (AD 185), said that St. Peter wrote it from Rome.

Other scholars say that Babylon refers to Egypt, especially since St. Peter said, "with Mark my son." Thus, some scholars said that Peter and Mark went to Egypt and that Peter wrote this letter from Egypt while St. Mark was with him. Not many people support this possibility, but I am just mentioning it because some scholars suggest that Babylon may refer to Egypt here, and that St. Peter wrote this letter from Egypt while he was with St. Mark; but as I said, not many fathers support this opinion.

GENERALLY

Some of the Epistles are called "Catholic Epistles." The word, "catholic," means universal. These epistles are called, the "Catholic Epistles," because they were not sent to a certain person or to a certain church, like St. Paul's letters (which were sent to a specific person or to a specific church).

There are some general letters, which we refer to as the "Catholic Epistles." These are the Epistle of St. James, the First and Second Epistles of St. Peter, the First, Second, and Third Epistles of St. John, and the Epistle of St. Jude. The First Epistle of St. Peter is one of these Catholic Epistles.

RECIPIENT OF THIS LETTER

Pilgrims of the Dispersion
We read in Chapter 1:1, the recipients are the "pilgrims of the Dispersion." The word, "dispersion," refers to those who were dispersed outside Jerusalem, in the rest of the whole world, especially after the Babylonian captivity and the Assyrian captivity. The word, "dispersion" is also found in the Holy Gospel according to St. John (7:35). It describes the Israelites, or the Jews, who were "scattered" following the Assyrian and Babylonian captivities.

Many thought that this letter was addressed only to the Jewish Christians because the word, "dispersion," cannot be applied, technically, to the Gentiles, because the Gentiles were not dispersed; they were not scattered. Thus, they said that this letter was only addressed to the Jews who were dispersed outside Jerusalem. Furthermore, St. James, in his letter, Chapter 1:1, said that he addressed his letter to the Jews in dispersion.

There is a reference to the Gentiles in Chapter 1 verse 14 in St. Peter's first letter, because he told them: "Your former life, before you believed in Christ." He was referring to the Gentiles here. We cannot say that St. Peter wrote his letter only to the Jews who were scattered, but he also wrote it to the Christians, both from a Jewish background and Gentiles who converted to Christianity.

Why did he refer to the Gentiles as the "dispersion," or "dispersed," when they were in their own countries? If you study the letters of St. Paul and St. Peter, many of the terms that were applied to the Jews were also applied to the Gentiles and the Christians. We can say that St. Peter applied the word, "dispersion," to all the Christians, as he applied it to the Church in general; other designations were formerly applied only to Israel. Thus, if a small part of the Church is called, "dispersion," we can use this description and generalize it to the whole Church.

Therefore, we can say that St. Peter's initial audience were Christian, whom he called, "pilgrims," and were living in five provinces in Asia Minor: Pontus, Galatia, Cappadocia, Asia, and Bithynia. These five provinces are in present-day Turkey. We read about this area in Acts, Chapter 16, that St. Paul preached in Asia Minor, especially in Bithynia, and he traveled in all these areas and preached the gospel there. Thus, this area was blessed by the preaching of St. Paul, and they also received a letter from St. Peter.

PURPOSE FOR WRITING THIS LETTER

As it is clear from many passages, the Christians in Asia Minor had experienced severe persecution. That is why St. Peter wrote to them, to encourage them and to support them in remaining steadfast during this persecution. In order to encourage them, he reminds them of their privileges in Christ, their blessings, and he also instructs them about their duties as Christians, as the elect of God, as His special people. Thus, he spoke to them about their salvation and their privileges. Then he explained to them how they should conduct themselves as the people of God, His own special people.

THEME

The theme of the epistle is: "Conduct becoming or befitting the people of God." It shows us how we should conduct ourselves, and how we should behave as His own special people, His own elect, His own children, and His own family.

OUTLINE

This letter is five chapters. St. Peter starts with the introduction and salutation; then, speaks about our salvation in Christ. After he spoke about our salvation in Christ, he spoke about our conduct and how we should conduct ourselves as children of God.

He explained our conduct in three views:

I. **In view of our privileges.** If we understand our privileges, we we should conduct ourselves accordingly.

II. **In view of our position.** Who are we in Christ? After we understand our position in Christ, we should conduct ourselves in such a way.

III. **In view of our persecution.** Now that we understand that persecution is something expected for Christians, how are we to conduct ourselves when there is persecution?

OUTLINE OF 1 PETER

Chapter 1
• Greeting to the elect pilgrims(1-2)
• A heavenly inheritance (3-12)
• Living before God our Father (13-21)
• The enduring word (22-25)
• Qualities needed in trials (19-20)
• Doers, not hearers only (21-27)

Chapter 2
• A call to spiritual growth (1-3)
• The chosen Stone and His chosen people (1-10)
• Living before the world (11-12)
• Submission to government (13-17)
• Submission to masters (18-25)

Chapter 3
• Submission to husands(1-6)
• A word to husbands (7)
• Called to blessing (8-12)
• Suffering for right and wrong (13-17)
• Christ's suffering and ours (18-22)

Chapter 4
• Our Duties as sufferers for righteousness' sake (1-6)
• Serving for God's glory (7-11)
• Suffering for God's glory (12-19)

Chapter 5
• Shepherd the flock (1-4)
• Submit to God, resist the devil (5-11)
• Farewell and peace (12-14)

1

Chapter Outline

- Greeting to the elect pilgrims(1-2)
- A heavenly inheritance (3-12)
- Living before God our Father (13-21)
- The enduring word (22-25)
- Qualities needed in trials (19-20)
- Doers, not hearers only (21-27)

Introduction

St. Peter begins his First Epistle to the Christians in Asia Minor by acknowledging their election. They were elected by God. He connects this election to the Holy Trinity, saying that they were elected according to the foreknowledge of God the Father, according to the economy of God the Father.

The Father elected us to be His children. How? This election was made possible by the work of the Holy Spirit in us, the sanctifying work of the Holy Spirit to obey the word of God. You cannot obey the commandment of God without the grace of the Holy Spirit. That is why God sent us the Holy Spirit to sanctify us and to empower us to obey His holy word. We cannot receive the Holy Spirit without the salvation that Jesus Christ performed on the cross, and without the sprinkling of the blood of Jesus Christ to redeem us and to save us.

We were elected to be the family of God, His children, heirs with Christ, and to fulfill this election, we must be sanctified by the Holy Spirit; but the Holy Spirit cannot sanctify us without the salvation performed by the Lord Jesus Christ on the Cross.

Here, we have the Holy Trinity:

- The Father elected us; chose us.
- The Son fulfilled salvation; and then,
- Through this salvation, the Holy Spirit now sanctified us, in order to obey the word of God and inherit the kingdom of God.

After this, St. Peter praises God for the living hope that we have received. This hope is living because it is founded in the resurrection of Christ—in the living resurrection of Christ. What is this living hope? This living hope is our inheritance. Now, he is comparing between earthly inheritance and heavenly inheritance. Earthly inheritance is corruptible, fades away, but heavenly inheritance is incorruptible, and not only incorruptible, but it is glorious; we will be glorified with Christ.

While some things may not decay but do not have glory, our inheritance is not only incorruptible, but it does not decay and is also glorious—salvation. We will be glorified as the Lord Jesus said in John 17:5, "And now, O Father, glorify Me together with Yourself, with the glory which I had with You before the world was." Our living hope, our incorruptible inheritance, and our glorious salvation will be revealed at the Second Coming of Christ.

Then, he acknowledged that we would go through difficult times on earth. There are trials, there is suffering, but this suffering, although not initiated by God, He will use it for our purification. Although this suffering is not initiated by God because death and suffering entered the world through the envy of the devil, God uses suffering for our purification.

And through the power of God, our faith is protected; and not only is our faith protected, but God will give us comfort and joy, as St. Peter described it as inexpressible joy, even amid suffering.

This salvation and this living hope were mentioned in the Scripture. At that time, in the first Century, people did not have the New Testament. The only Scripture they had was the Old Testament. That is why he told them, "If you read the prophecies, if you read the Scripture, if you read the Old Testament, you will find that many prophets prophesied about this incorruptible inheritance, this glorious salvation, this living hope." The fact that the prophets prophesied about this means that they were inspired by the Holy Spirit; the Holy Spirit led them and inspired them

in writing about this salvation.

After that, St. Peter tells them, "Now that you understand your privilege and who you are in Christ, you are saved, you are appointed and elected for an incorruptible inheritance, a glorious salvation, a living hope. So, let me tell you, in view of this salvation, in view of this privilege, how you should conduct yourselves as the family of God, as His own special people, as His own children."

(1) You need to focus your mind and hope on the grace that we will receive in the Second Coming of Christ. (2) Do not set your mind on earthly things but set your mind on heavenly and eternal things, because whatever is here on earth is perishable and will fade away. Thus, it is not wise to set your mind on earthly things.

Now, if you understand your privilege and if you understand this salvation that will be revealed in the Second Coming of Christ, you should be preoccupied with this. As obedient children to God, you should be like God. God is holy, and you need to be holy. You need to fear and revere God.

Also, keep in mind that God will judge us without partiality. Keeping this in mind, that we will stand before the throne of God and give an account, we should walk in the fear of God, in holiness, and in becoming like Him and growing in being transformed into the image of His Son.

Furthermore, when the Holy Spirit purifies your heart, He [the Holy Spirit] that fills your heart will bear the fruit of love. That is why, as Christians, you should love one another fervently with pure hearts. The work of the Holy Spirit in our hearts will bear the fruit of love, and we will love one another with sincerity from a pure heart.

Especially that we are now born again of the Holy Spirit [through the Holy Mysteries of Baptism and Chrismation] by the incorruptible word of God, we should be different than the children of the world. The children of the world who are not born again cannot have this love, which is the fruit of the Holy Spirit; but we who are born again of the Holy Spirit in the Holy Mystery of Baptism, we are able to love one another with sincerity.

––––––––––

1:1 **Peter, an apostle of Jesus Christ, to the pilgrims of the Dispersion in Pontus, Galatia, Cappadocia, Asia, and Bithynia.** Like all the apostolic epistles, whether the letters of St. Paul or the letters of James or John, this epistle starts with introducing the author: "Peter, an apostle of Jesus Christ." When he said,

"an apostle," notice that he did not claim any superiority. He did not say, "the chief apostle or the prime apostle," as the Catholic Church claims the primacy of Peter; he said, "an apostle of the Lord Jesus Christ."

As I explained earlier, he is addressing both the Jewish and Gentile Christians in this epistle. He uses the word "dispersion" to refer to the Jewish people outside Judea, but he used this term generally, to include all the Christians. This letter is directed to the churches in the five provinces of the Roman Empire in Asia Minor (located in modern-day Turkey): Pontus, Galatia, Cappadocia, Asia, and Bithynia.

1:2 **elect according to the foreknowledge of God the Father, in sanctification of the Spirit, for obedience and sprinkling of the blood of Jesus Christ.** Now, he is speaking about their election and their salvation. When we speak about election, some denominations understand that God elected some people and did not elect others; but no. God actually chose every single person in the whole world who believes in Him. The election is for everybody, but it is your choice whether to accept this election or to reject it.

God made a plan to save everybody and to choose everyone to join His family, to be His own special people. This plan was in God's mind before the foundation of the world. That is why he said, "the foreknowledge of God."

God elected everybody, and part of this election is that He knew we would go through suffering, but He uses this suffering for our purification, although He does not initiate it, as St. Peter will explain. This election and salvation were in accordance with God's purpose to save us—to save all human beings.

How was this election and salvation made possible? After the fall, corruption and sin and death entered the world. Since we cannot inherit the kingdom of God with this corruption, and we cannot inherit the kingdom of God while we are mortal, we needed to be sanctified, to be immortal, and to be without corruption to inherit the kingdom of God. That is why God gave us the Holy Spirit.

After we are baptized in this Holy Mystery and confirmed in the Holy Mystery of Confirmation [Chrismation], we receive the Holy Spirit to come and abide in us, "You are the temple of God and the Holy Spirit abides in you" (1 Cor. 3:16). The Holy Spirit in me purifies me, sanctifies me, and empowers me to obey the word of God and, thus, actually qualifies me to this inheritance, to this election. I cannot do it by myself; I am only able to do it through the grace of the Holy Spirit.

Not only through the Holy Spirit who is within me, but also the Holy Spirit who is working in the whole Church through the Mysteries of the Church. God gave the Holy Spirit to me, to every baptized and confirmed Christian, and He also gave the Holy Spirit to the Church, to work through the Church through the Mysteries. Therefore, we are also sanctified through the Church, being members in the family of God and through the Mysteries of the Church.

What is the purpose of this sanctification? St. Peter said, it is for obedience, to be able to obey the commandments of God and, thus, you will be able to inherit the kingdom of God.

I told you about the Holy Spirit that we receive Him in chrismation after baptism, but what is baptism? Baptism is participation in the death and resurrection of Christ. It is impossible to receive the Holy Spirit without the death and resurrection of Christ. That is why God did not send the Holy Spirit except after the death and resurrection of Christ and His ascension. That is why this sanctification was made possible through the sprinkling of the blood of the Lord Jesus Christ.

In this verse, we see the work of the Holy Trinity. God the Father chose us, appointed us for this salvation, elected us, and the Son redeemed us by His blood, and through His blood, and now the Holy Spirit sanctifies us in order to obey the word of God. That is why St. Peter said we were elected according to the foreknowledge of God the Father, in sanctification of the Spirit for obedience, to obey the word of God, and sprinkling of the blood of Jesus Christ.

Grace to you and peace be multiplied. Most of the apostles used this salutation: grace and peace, peace and grace … "Grace to you and peace be multiplied." The most needed gifts are grace and peace. Grace, because without the grace of God, we cannot do anything; we will be failures—total failures. It is only through the grace of God that we can be successful in our lives.

In this world, we will have many, many tribulations, and we cannot withstand all these sufferings without the peace of God—"the peace of God, which surpasses all understanding" (Phil 4:7). That is why all the apostles in their letters started by saying, "Grace and peace, or peace and grace," and this grace is the source of peace in our hearts, so he tells them, "Grace to you and peace be multiplied."

I think it is a good prayer when you pray for yourself, when you pray for your children, when you pray for your family, when you pray for your friends, when you pray for your enemies, to ask God to give us His grace and His peace, as St. Peter said, "Grace to you and peace be multiplied."

1:3 **Blessed be the God and Father of our Lord Jesus Christ, who according to His abundant mercy has begotten us again to a living hope through the resurrection of Jesus Christ from the dead.** After St. Peter spoke about our salvation and our election, he understands very, very well that this salvation and election is not because we are worthy, and is not because we deserve it, but it is because of His abundant mercy. That is why he gave thanksgiving to God the Father, because without His mercy, we would not be saved.

We are not worthy to be saved. We do not deserve it. We rebel against God. That is why he begins by saying, "Blessed be the God and Father of our Lord Jesus Christ, who according to His abundant mercy," because it is out of His overflowing mercy, not out of our worthiness, that has caused us to be born again as His children.

has begotten us again. "Again," because the first birth is the biological birth from our parents—the physical birth, but for Christians, we are now born again, not by a physical birth but a spiritual birth, as the Lord said to Nicodemus in John 3:6, "That which is born of the flesh is flesh, and that which is born of the Spirit is spirit."

When he uses the words, "begotten us," it means we have become His children. This is very important because who is eligible to inherit? Only children! To inherit the kingdom of God, we must be His children. That is why we were born again as His children. Therefore, we are now heirs of the kingdom of heaven and heirs with Christ.

We are born again in baptism, as the Lord said to Nicodemus, "Unless you are born again of water and Spirit, you cannot enter the kingdom of God" (cf. John 3) Why can you not enter? Without being born again, you are not His children, and if you are not His children, you are ineligible for inheritance.

to a living hope through the resurrection of Jesus Christ from the dead. This hope—we are not just telling you a fable or a story or something superstitious. No. It is reality. This hope is a living hope and it is a real hope, because this hope is founded upon the resurrection of Jesus Christ.

St. Peter, as a witness of the sufferings of Christ and as a witness of His resurrection, knows that this hope is a living hope. As Jesus rose from the dead, we will be risen from the dead and inherit the kingdom of God. That is why as children, born again Christians (through the Holy Mysteries of Baptism and Chrismation), have hope of the inheritance of eternal life, and this hope is founded upon the resurrection of the Lord Jesus Christ from the dead.

This hope is not just a hope of mere eternal existence, that we will live for eternity but, no, it is more than this; we will become heirs of God, heirs with Christ, glorified with Christ, and as real children of God, fully adopted by God. That is why in verse 4 he said:

1:4 to an inheritance incorruptible and undefiled and that does not fade away, reserved in heaven for you. The word, "inheritance," only befits children. This inheritance is incorruptible. It never decays. It is totally different from an earthly inheritance. An earthly inheritance is corruptible, but this inheritance is incorruptible; it can never decay.

and undefiled. It is sinless. It is eternal It cannot be defiled like an earthly inheritance.

to an inheritance incorruptible and undefiled and that does not fade away. The third characteristic of this inheritance is that it does not fade away. Maybe if I had inherited some money from my parents, it would fade away; but an eternal inheritance never fades away. It is reserved; it is eternal.

reserved in heaven for you This inheritance is reserved for those who believed in Christ, who accepted His election, and God has reserved this inheritance in heaven for us so that when we go to heaven, we will receive this inheritance.

1:5 who are kept by the power of God through faith for salvation ready to be revealed in the last time. Maybe Satan will attack you with some doubts: "What if I lose this inheritance? What if I commit many, many sins, and I lose the inheritance?" St. Peter is assuring us: "You are preserved; you are kept by the power of God."

The grace of the Holy Spirit that I received in the Mystery of Chrismation protects me, sanctifies me, purifies me, convicts me, and when I sin, forgives me and moves me from death to life. That is why he tells us, "Who are kept by the power of God." Do not be afraid; you are kept by the power of God through faith.

We accepted the Lord Jesus Christ and we believed in Him. Through this faith, we are protected, and we are kept by the power of God. If we endure to the end, and if this faith is steadfast even in the time of sufferings and trials, the protection of God will be to the end, in order to receive the salvation that is ready to be revealed in the last time.

The full salvation will be revealed in the Second Coming of Christ. So, now we have received the promise of salvation, but the full salvation, is when we receive the incorruptible inheritance, which will be in the Second Coming of Christ. That is why he said, "for salvation ready to be revealed in the last time." The "last time" refers to the Second Coming of Christ.

1:6 In this you greatly rejoice, though now for a little while, if need be, you have been grieved by various trials. When you think about this incorruptible inheritance, this glorious salvation which will never decay, which will never fade away, which will never be defiled, you will have joy in your hearts, and it is in this glorious hope that we rejoice. This joy will remain even amid the trials and suffering that we receive in the world.

That is why he told them, "you greatly rejoice, though now for a little while, if need be, you have been grieved by various trials," which indicates that the persecution of Christians had already started when he wrote this letter. These trials put our faith and our patience to test, but as St. James said, "Blessed is the man who endures temptation," (Jas 1:12) and "… who endures to the end," (James Chapter 5), and as the Lord Jesus Christ said, "But he that shall endure unto the end, the same shall be saved" (Mt 24:13). Thus, one of the purposes of these trials is to test our faith and patience.

1:7 that the genuineness of your faith, being much more precious than gold that perishes, though it is tested by fire, may be found to praise, honor, and glory at the revelation of Jesus Christ. Now, he is saying, "These trials will test your faith." Test your faith in what way? It is a way to purify my faith, and to purify me. St. Peter made a nice comparison here with gold. How do you purify gold from its impurities? You put it in fire. So, he said, "Your faith is actually more precious than gold, because gold perishes, but your faith is imperishable."

If gold is purified with fire, then you need to look at suffering as a way of purifying your faith, that the genuineness of your faith may be revealed. As gold is purified through fire, in the same way, the fire of trials will produce the fruits of "praise, honor, and glory at the revelation of Jesus Christ," that in His Second Coming we will praise, we will honor, and we will glorify Him.

Thus, these persecutions test our faith as gold is tested by fire, and the faith which stands the test, the faith which endures to the end, because it is more precious than gold, will bear the fruit. Which fruit? It will bear the fruit of praise and honor and glory at the appearing of the Lord Jesus Christ in His Second Coming

1:8 **whom (referring to Jesus) you love. Though now you do not see Him, yet believing, you rejoice with joy inexpressible and full of glory.** Peter saw the Lord Jesus Christ. He had this privilege, but the Gentiles did not see the Lord Jesus Christ. So, he told

them, "whom you have not seen with your physical eyes, but you saw Him with your hearts." "Blessed are the pure in heart for they shall see God." (Mt 5:8). That is why we love Him. We love Him because He loved us, and He redeemed us from our sins.

whom having not seen you love. Though now you do not see Him, yet believing. When you believe in Him, when you trust Him, you will see Him with your pure heart; then, seeing Him with your heart will bring joy to your heart. This joy is inexpressible and full of glory.

Though now you do not see Him, yet believing, you rejoice with joy inexpressible and full of glory. Though not having seen Christ, they know Him by faith, and they love Him. And because they believe in Him, they are now filled with this unspeakable joy of a glorious hope.

What is the fruit of the Spirit in us? It is mentioned in Galatians 5:22–23: "love, joy…," and this joy—the depth of this joy cannot be explained by anybody. That is why he said, "inexpressible and full of glory," because you cannot describe this joy. It is beyond description.

1:9 **receiving the end of your faith—the salvation of your souls.** Why do we believe? Why do we follow

Christ? Why did we accept Him to be our Lord, our King, our Savior, our Messiah? Why? The goal or the object of our faith is salvation. The object of the gospel is our salvation. That is why he said, "Why do you rejoice? Because you will receive the goal of your faith, which is salvation."

What is the goal of studying? What is the goal of going to school? The goal is to get a degree. When a student thinks about the degree that he will receive, his heart is full of joy. In the same way, when we think about the end of our faith, which is the salvation of our souls, this fills our hearts with inexpressible joy.

1:10 Of this salvation the prophets have inquired and searched carefully, who prophesied of the grace that would come to you. In the Old Testament, prophets like Isaiah, Jeremiah, and Daniel, wrote many things by the inspiration of the Holy Spirit, without understanding them. Maybe this was clear in the prophecy of Daniel because He wrote many things; yet, he said, "And I did not understand." God even sent Archangel Gabriel to Daniel to explain, but he said, "And I did not understand." It was a mystery.

They wrote things, but they did not understand. They prophesied about salvation, about the birth of Christ, about His crucifixion, about His resurrection,

about the salvation that was given to us. Thus, St. Peter is saying, "Of this salvation, the prophets have inquired and searched carefully. They wrote about it and they inquired in order to understand what they had written. They searched carefully to understand the meaning of what they wrote. These are the prophets who prophesied of the grace that would come to you." Thus, the prophets used words and symbols by the inspiration of the Spirit, but they did not comprehend the full meaning.

1:11 searching what or what manner of time, the Spirit of Christ who was in them was indicating when He testified beforehand the sufferings of Christ and the glories that would follow. What were they inquiring about? What were they searching carefully for? He gave us some examples: They were searching as to the time and in which specific era the Messiah would come, like in the Book of Daniel. There are any calculations about the birth of Christ. Thus, they were searching for what or what manner of time the Messiah would come.

Or what manner of time. This means, by what marks will distinguish this time? What are the marks? It is like right now; we inquire when Christ will return and what will be the signals of His coming? We do not know, but some people search; in the same way, the prophets were searching what time and what manner of time. "What manner of time," means, what are the marks to distinguish this time?

The Spirit of Christ. That is to say, the Holy Spirit who was in them was indicating, so, they were trying to understand what the Holy Spirit was indicating to them. In verse 11, he is saying, "The Spirit of Christ, the Holy Spirit in the prophets, indicated to them some prophesies about the sufferings of Christ, about the glories—like His resurrection and His ascension that would follow, and about our salvation. However, they did not understand what the time would be and what the marks of the time would be, and that is why they started to search."

The prophets of the Old Testament spoke of Christ and of His salvation and diligently inquired what the Spirit of Christ in them meant by these words. They spoke about the sufferings of Christ but could not understand these predictions. They could not understand these predictions.

1:12 **To them it was revealed that, not to themselves, but to us they were ministering the things which now have been reported to you through those who have preached the gospel to you by the Holy Spirit sent from heaven— things which angels desire to look into.**

To them. This refers to the prophets. The Holy Spirit did not leave them searching and inquiring. The Holy Spirit did not leave them in confusion. The Holy Spirit told them, "It is not for you to know the answers to these questions. You are not writing these things for yourselves. You are writing for generations to come who will receive these blessings."

That is why St. Peter said, "To them (to the prophets) it was revealed, by the Holy Spirit, that it was not to themselves that they were writing, but to us they were ministering (as they were writing) the things which now have been reported to you. These are the things that we now understand, the things that the apostles preached to us—like St. Peter, St. Paul, and St. Mark, that have been reported to you."

through those who have preached the gospel to you. The apostles, like St. Paul, St. Mark, St. Peter, the twelve disciples, and the seventy-two apostles, preached the gospel to you, "by the Holy Spirit sent from heaven." On the Day of Pentecost, they received the power of the Holy Spirit; then, they preached the gospel.

The prophets learned that all these predictions and prophecies were not written for them but were written for us in future time. Now, in the gospel of the New Testament, we have come to understand these prophecies.

Now, when we read Psalm 22 about the crucifixion of the Lord Jesus Christ, we understand. David did not understand it. Now we understand Psalm 22, verse 16, when he says, "They pierced my hands and my feet." Now, we understand this.

Therefore, the things that he mentioned here, the things which now have been reported (he means the gospel), reported to you through those (referring to the apostles, like St. Paul and his companions who preached under the influence of the Holy Spirit), under the inspiration of the Holy Spirit preached to us the mysteries of the gospel.

One of these Holy Sacraments is the Mystery of the Communion [the Holy Eucharist]. Can you imagine that God is with us by His body and His blood on the altar every day? During Communion, the deacons chant a hymn called, "Pioik" (ⲡⲓⲱⲓⲕ—meaning, "The Bread [of life])." In this hymn, we say: "The angels who are standing before the throne of God cover their faces with their wings. They cannot behold His glory," but we can see Him every day on the altar.

We have privileges that even the angels do not have. The angels cannot behold the glory of God, but we see Him every day with us on the altar. That is why St. Peter said, "things which angels desire to look into."

In the festal, long hymn of "Greet one another" (referring to the long chant by the deacon during the Prayer of Reconciliation in the Divine Liturgy), we say that the angels cover their faces because of the awesome glory of God, but as for us, we see Him every day on the altar.

St. Peter is explaining to us the greatness of the privileges that we have received. We have received what many prophets and righteous men desired to see but did not see, and we have received things that many prophets and righteous men desired to hear but did not hear, and we have even received Mysteries and blessings that the angels desire to behold but have not. Let us know how great the privileges are we have received.

1:13 Therefore gird up the loins of your mind, be sober, and rest your hope fully upon the grace that is to be brought to you at the revelation of Jesus Christ. Now, he will explain to us what our conduct and behavior ought to be in view of these privileges. If you understand all the privileges that you have received, in what manner should you conduct yourself?

That is why he said, "Therefore having such encouragement, after having understood all these privileges, gird up the loins of your mind." There was a custom where they girded their loins when they started to work or when they started a journey. St. Peter is using the same symbol or expression of "girding the loins," telling them to gird the loins of their minds, to be ready. Prepare your mind because the transformation starts with the renewal of your mind. Be transformed by the renewal of your mind. Prepare yourself for this journey.

Gird up the loins of your mind, be sober. Be watchful. Let there be sobriety of the spirit—of your spirit. "Be watchful," as he said, "Because our enemy the devil is like a roaring lion and wants us to be powerless."

and rest your hope fully upon the grace that is to be brought to you at the revelation of Jesus Christ. If you start to feel fainthearted think about this living hope. This hope is a confident hope. Never let your hope cease but set your mind on this hope. This hope will motivate you. This hope will encourage you. This hope which will be revealed at the Second Coming of Christ. Set your hope fully upon the grace, this grace of salvation that is to be brought to you at the revelation of Jesus Christ.

1:14 as obedient children, not conforming yourselves to the former lusts, as in your ignorance. You are born again; so, now you are children. What is the duty of children toward their parents? Obedience. In the same way, now that we are the children

of God, what should we do? We should obey God. Obedience is a characteristic of Christians because Christians are the children of God.

St. Peter is saying, "Now, you understand your privilege. You are the children of God. Now, in view of this privilege, since you are children, as obedient children, do not conform yourselves to the former lusts, as in your former ignorance." He is speaking to the Gentiles, here, when they did not believe in Christ, when they did not worship the God of Israel. This is the ignorance that is meant here. Ignorance means they did not know God; they were worshiping idols.

"But now you are children, do not conform yourselves to the former lusts, to the previous behavior before believing in Christ, because at that time, you were not children of God; you were children of the world, but now you are children of God."

The difference between God's children and the children of the world is the commandment of God—the obedience to the commandments of God. This obedience will turn me away from my former sins, the sins I have practiced before believing in Christ, or before repenting and living my Christian faith.

1:15 but as He who called you is holy, you also be holy in all your

conduct. Do you remember who called us? It is God the Father, as St. Peter said in verse 2, "according to the foreknowledge of God the Father we were elected." So, "as He who called you is holy, you also be holy in all your conduct." Children are like their parents, so as our Father is holy, we also should be holy. God who called us is holy. As we became His children we should be in the likeness of our heavenly Father. It is our calling to be holy in every conduct.

This verse is like a commandment: Be holy; live a holy life. However, as I previously mentioned, since you cannot obey without the grace of the Holy Spirit, there is also a promise here: "If you abide in the Holy Spirit and if you live according to the grace of the Holy Spirit in you, My promise to you is I will transform you to be holy as I am holy." This passage has a promise and a commandment. The promise is that God will sanctify us and will make us holy as He is holy, and the commandment is that we need to obey His word.

1:16 **because it is written, "Be holy, for I am holy."** This is written in the Book of Leviticus, 11:44 and 19:2. Thus, we not only obey the commandment of God, but we should also seek to imitate His holiness, to be holy as He is holy, for it is written, "Be holy, for I am holy."

1:17 **And if you call on the Father, who without partiality judges according to each one's work, conduct yourselves throughout the time of your stay here in fear.** Every time we pray, we say, "Our Father who art in heaven." If you call on Him, you should know that you will give account; you will be judged. You call Him "Father" and He is also the Judge, and in His judgment, He does not show any partiality.

St. Peter says to conduct our lives here on earth in the fear of God, but fear does not mean to be scared or terrified of God, but to revere Him. Out of reverence to Him, we are to obey Him, to imitate Him, to be holy as He is holy.

God judges us according to our works, according to our deeds, as we say in the Divine Liturgy, "He appointed a day for recompense in which He will appear to judge the world in righteousness and give each one according to his deeds." Thus, we will be judged according to our deeds. There is no partiality. God will not judge us according to our race or our social status. No. He will judge us according to our deeds.

If you seek His blessings and promises, walk in the fear of God. What is the beginning of wisdom? The beginning of wisdom is the fear of God, as we read in Proverbs and in other Scripture (cf. Prov. 1:7, 9:10; Ps 111:10). So, why do you need to be holy? Because you will be judged. You will give an account. Without holiness, as St. Paul said in Hebrews 12:14, nobody can see God. Therefore, we need to be holy to inherit the kingdom of God.

St. Peter says, "Conduct yourselves throughout the time of your stay here [on earth]"—meaning that our lives here is like a period of sojourn. We are on a journey. Thus, during our lives here on earth, we need to conduct ourselves in the fear of God.

worshiped idols as their parents did, and in the same way, the Jews rejected Christ as their parents rejected Christ.

But now, God has redeemed us not by gold or silver. He redeemed us by His blood. Gold and silver are perishable, but His blood is more precious than gold and silver. "Knowing that you were not redeemed with corruptible things, like silver or gold, from your aimless [fruitless] conduct received by tradition [by learning] from your fathers [from your parents]."

1:18 **Knowing that you were not redeemed with corruptible things, like silver or gold, from your aimless conduct received by tradition from your fathers.** When they put someone in prison, he can be released on bail by payment of some money. Thus, St. Peter is saying, "You were not redeemed with gold or silver; these things are corruptible, but you were redeemed from your aimless conduct, from your fruitless behavior." How were you redeemed? By the blood of Jesus Christ; gold or earthly wealth could never redeem us, forgive our sins, or purify us.

St. Peter describes their former conduct as "aimless." Aimless means fruitless, has no profit; it is vain—vanity. He tells them that they received it by tradition from their fathers. Whether they are Jews or Gentiles, they all learned all this bad behavior from their parents—from their fathers. For example, the Gentiles

1:19 **but with (you were redeemed with) the precious blood of Christ, as of a lamb without blemish and without spot.** Jesus offered Himself as a Lamb, our Passover Lamb. He died on the cross to redeem us. Christ is the Lamb of God who took away our sins in His body and died on the cross to redeem us. Therefore, understand: you were redeemed with the precious blood of Christ, the Lamb of God, who is the Lamb without blemish, the Lamb without spot, sinless, because unless He was sinless, He could not have redeemed us. He is the sinless Lamb.

1:20 **He indeed was foreordained before the foundation of the world, but was manifest in these last times for you.** "He," referring to Jesus Christ, "was foreordained." God the Father, when He chose us for salvation, when He elected us for salvation, appointed His Son to be our Redeemer. This ordination, this appointment, was from before the foundation of the world. He, Jesus, was indeed foreordained, appointed before the foundation of the world to be the Lamb of God, to be our Passover Lamb.

Thus, the Lord Jesus Christ was the center of the Father's plan of salvation from the beginning, but this plan was manifested to us during His incarnation. That is why St. Peter said, "but was manifest in these last times for you." Although Christ was foreordained by the Father even from before the foundation of the world, He was manifested in the last times.

Why did St. Peter call it the "last times?" It is because it was the end of the Jewish age and the end of the Temple—the destruction of the Temple. That is why he described this time as "these last times for you." Thus, Christ was manifested for the sake of God's people who have become God's people by believing in Christ.

1:21 **who through Him believe in God, who raised Him from the dead and gave Him glory, so that your faith and hope are in God.** Through Jesus Christ, we believe in God the Father. Jesus told us, "Nobody has seen the Father, but the Son who is in the bosom of the Father revealed Him to us" (John 1:18). How did we hear about the Father? We heard about the Father through the Son. He told us, "Nobody can come to the Father except through me" (John 14:6). That is why St. Peter said, "who through Him [through Jesus], believe in God." Through Jesus, we now believe in the Father who raised Him [Jesus] from the dead.

When we speak about the resurrection, there are some verses that say, "The Father raised Jesus from the dead," and other verses say, "Jesus rose from the dead by Himself," and still other verses that say, "The Holy Spirit raised Him from the dead;" so the resurrection is the work of the Holy Trinity. That is why when St. Peter said, "who [the Father] raised Him from the dead," because the resurrection like any other divine work, is the work of the Holy Trinity together.

who raised Him from the dead and gave Him glory. The Father gave Jesus glory after His (Christ's) ascension. He (Jesus Christ) was seated at the right hand of the Father so that your faith and hope are in God, in the Father. Now, we believe in the Father who raised Jesus and gave Him glory. Our faith in God is that as He raised Jesus, we also will be raised, and our hope in Him is a living hope.

Therefore, the Lord Jesus Christ was manifested for us, for our sake, to make us the people of God through believing in Him, the Father. Our faith and our hope proceed from the power of His resurrection, from His victory over death. Our faith in the Father and our hope in the Father are based on the resurrection, as St. Paul said, "If Jesus did not rise from the dead, your faith is in vain." (1 Cor 15:14)

gave Him glory. At His ascension. Without Christ, we fear the Father; we dread Him. However, through Jesus, we believe in the Father, we love the Father, and we have hope in the Father.

1:22 **Since you have purified your souls in obeying the truth through the Spirit in sincere love of the brethren, love one another fervently with a pure heart.** Now, he is saying that as children, you should be obedient, and by obeying the word of God, you have this purification. Now, you are purified in obeying the truth through the Spirit, the Holy Spirit who works in you and me to purify us through the Mysteries of the Church.

In sincere love of the brethren. Now, I will bear the fruit of the Holy Spirit, which is love—"love one another fervently with a pure heart." The word "purified"—"Since you have purified"—in Greek, this verb was mentioned seven times in the New Testament. Four of those times it was referring to ceremonial purification and three times it was referring to moral purification, which is to cleanse us from our sins.

Therefore, when St. Peter said, "Since you have purified," he is not referring only to that our sins are forgiven, but also how we are to live a pure and holy life—the positive aspect of it, not only the forgiveness of sins, but the positive aspect of it.

This purification comes through obeying the word of God and through the work of the Holy Spirit through the Mysteries of the Church. That is why he said, "you have purified your souls in obeying the truth through the Spirit," because when you obey the word of God, when you are baptized and when you receive the Holy Spirit, the Holy Spirit will purify your heart. And now, you will bear the fruit of the Holy Spirit, which is love. Thus, since you have purified your heart, in sincere love of the brethren, love one another.

The children of God should love one another. The fruit of the Holy Spirit is brotherly love. How can you say, "I am Christian," without loving your brethren for whom Jesus died on the cross? How can you say you are Christian, and you are from the children of God? God is love. If you do not have this love with sincerity in your heart, you are not from His children. If He is love, you should also have this sincere love in your heart. That is why he used the words, "fervently with a pure heart"—from a pure heart.

1:23 **having been born again, not of corruptible seed but incorruptible, through the word of God which lives and abides.** St. Peter is again reminding us of our privilege: You were born again, and you are purified You were born again in baptism and your rebirth was not of corruptible seed. When we were born from our parents, we were born in sin: "And in sin my mother conceived me" (Psalm 51:5), and we die, but the rebirth of the Spirit is not of corruptible seed but is incorruptible. We are born of the Spirit of God and He is incorruptible.

How are we born again? It is through the word of God. What makes the water of baptism? What gives the water of baptism the power of rebirth? The priest prays many, many prayers over the water, so the water is blessed by the word of God. Now, this water, when the Spirit of God descends upon it through the word of God and through the prayers, it gives us this rebirth. We are born again from water and Spirit.

That is why he said, "having been born again, not of corruptible seed but incorruptible, through the word of God which lives and abides forever," because the corruptible seed dies, but the word of God lives and abides forever. The word of God is a living word because it is written by the Holy Spirit. The word of God pierces my heart, moves my heart, and has power to change my heart.

In Hebrews 4:12, St. Paul says: "It is sharper than a two-edged sword;" It has life in itself. That is why it communicates life to me, and that is why he described the word of God as that "which lives and abides forever." God's word lives forever.

1:24 **because 'All flesh is as grass, And all the glory of man as the flower of the grass. The grass withers, And its flower falls away.** Now, he is comparing between being born again of the word of God and being born of flesh—born of Spirit versus born of flesh, and he quotes Isaiah 40. What he is saying here is, "When you were born from your parents, from flesh, you were born of corruptible seed, and this corruptible seed, this flesh, is like the grass, and earthly glory is like the flower of the grass. When the sun rises the grass will wither away and the flower will fade away. But, if you are born of the Spirit in baptism, if you are born of the word of God," let us see what Isaiah 40 says in the next verse, verse 25:

1:25 **But the word of the Lord endures forever.' Now this is the word which by the gospel was preached to you.** The fleshly life is like grass, soon followed by death, but if you are born from the living and eternal word, you are born to live forever, to be immortal; it is a birth to eternal life. This word is like its Author, God. This word is eternal and never loses its power—"the word of the Lord endures forever."

Now this is the word which by the gospel was preached to you. This is the word of the gospel. This is the word of God, which was preached to us by the apostles. That is why the more I study the word of God, the more it will purify me.

When I keep the word of God in my heart, as David said, "I hid your word in my heart lest I sin against You" (Psalm 119:11). This is the power of the word of God. It is sharper than a two-edged sword. It purifies me, cleanses me, and it will also give me eternal life, not to be defiled or corrupted.

Chapter 1 Questions

1. What does St. Paul mean when he refers to the pilgrims of Dispersion as "elect according to the foreknowledge of the Father"?

2. Identify the three persons of the Holy Trinity in 1 Peter 1:2. In what way is each member of the Godhead described?

3. In 1 Peter 1:3, what kind of hope are we asked to have? Why?

4. If God already knows how we will stand under trial, why does He choose to test our faith?

5. What did the Old Testament prophets search carefully to find?

6. How can the statement, "Be holy, for I am holy," be understood as both a command and a promise?

7. What does it mean to conduct ourselves in fear?

8. What is the incorruptible seed through which we are born again? In what way are we born again?

2

Chapter Outline

Introduction

St. Peter concluded Chapter 1 by saying that, in baptism, you were born again, and because you are now born by a spiritual birth from God, you are now the children of God. He starts Chapter 2 by asking the people to put aside sinful attitudes and to grow spiritually. He tells them that as infants desire pure milk to grow (the baby desires milk, which is an essential element for his growth), so, we Christians, when we are born again in baptism, should desire the pure milk of the word of God, which is the Scripture. The word of God will help us to grow.

Then, he tells them, "When you accepted Christ, you came to Him as a Living Stone," and he used this description of Christ because describing Christ as a stone or as a rock is a common description, as we read in many prophecies, referring to Him as being a cornerstone, the foundation upon which we build our spiritual lives. Thus, St. Peter told them, and is telling us, "You also became living stones in this spiritual building which is called the House of God, or the Church."

Now that you know you do not have a lasting house here on earth, but your home is in heaven, so here on earth, you are sojourners and pilgrims in this world, and that is why you should conduct yourself in a way that befits your calling as children of God.

This should be reflected in our behaviors and he gave some examples of how we should submit to authorities, how even the slaves should submit to their masters, not only to the good and kind, but to the harsh, and he gave them reasons why they should submit.

2:1 **Therefore, laying aside all malice, all deceit, hypocrisy, envy, and all evil speaking**. "Therefore," means, in view of salvation, in view of the rebirth that you obtained in baptism, you need to show brotherly love to one another, as he said in Chapter 1:22. Now you are born again; you are Christians. The main point of Christianity is love, because God is love. Since we are His children, we should have this love in our hearts—our love to God and our love to the brethren.

That is why when the Lord Jesus Christ was asked about what the greatest commandment was, He said, "Love the Lord your God and love your neighbor as yourself" (cf. Luke 10:27). This is the summary of all the commandments and the whole Scripture.

St. Peter is telling them, "In view of this salvation, and now that you understand your responsibility as Christians to show this brotherly love, you need to lay aside malice, deceit, hypocrisy, envy, and all evil speaking."

He also mentions five things that are contrary or inconsistent with brotherly love. You cannot say, "I love my brother, or I love my neighbor," if you possess one of these five characteristics. What are these?

(1) **Malice:** What is malice? Malice is the mental state opposed to love. Malice is to plan in sneaky ways to hurt others. That is malice, which is contrary to brotherly love.

(2) **Deceit:** It is the opposite of sincerity. Deceit is the betrayal of others, like how Judas betrayed the Lord Jesus Christ. Deceit is the opposite of sincerity and faithfulness.

(3) **Hypocrisy:** It is the external form of deceit. It is how deceit is shown in words and deeds and actions. Deceit is like an attitude in the heart, and hypocrisy is the external form of deceit shown in words and works.

(4) **Envy:** Envy is when you desire what others have. Envy starts by focusing on what you are lacking. Then, you become resentful and jealous desiring what others possess that you are lack. Instead of counting your blessings, you are focused on what you do not have. Nobody in the world has everything; nobody has everything. If you want to look at what you are lacking, you will find it. This will trigger envy of others. But we read in 1 Corinthians 13:4 that love does not envy. If you have this brotherly love in your heart, you will not envy others.

(5) **Evil Speaking:** The last point is evil speaking. Gossip and speaking evil of one another behind peoples' backs is what Christians should not do.

Thus, St. Peter is saying, "Therefore, considering your salvation, in light of your rebirth as a Christian, you need to put away malice, deceit, hypocrisy, envy, and evil speaking."

2:2 as newborn babes, desire the pure milk of the word, that you may grow thereby. He said, "You are born twice: the first is the physical birth from our parents, and the second is that you were also born again from the water and Spirit in baptism. As a baby desires milk, so you who are babes in Christ, desire the pure milk as newborn babes do." In Chapter 1:23, he spoke about our new birth in baptism as babes hunger for milk. Thus, he is saying, "You, as newborn babes in Christ, you need to earnestly desire the sincere and pure milk of the word."

St. Peter uses the word, "pure," to describe the word of God because many people, when interpreting the word of God, adulterate the word of God and cheat the word of God because of their personal interpretation. That is why he is asking us to understand the word of God in the same way that God intended it.

When God sent us His word, He intended a certain message and a certain interpretation of each word, and we, in order to grow, should reach this understanding, this interpretation. That is why he said, "the pure."

The word of God unchanged and unadulterated is the food on which all Christians must feed in order to grow, which means that if you do not study the Scripture, if you do not read the Scripture and keep it in your heart, if you do not practice and live by the word of God, you are not growing spiritually.

As a child who does not drink milk cannot grow, in the same way, if you do not read the word of God, if you do not keep the word of God in your heart, if you do not practice and live by the word of God, you are not growing spiritually. St. Peter says, "That you may grow thereby."

2:3 If indeed you have tasted that the Lord is gracious. Have you really tasted God's graciousness? How? You taste that the Lord is gracious because He saved us out of His goodness, not because we are worthy. He saved us out of His mercies, not because we deserve it. People who have tasted that the Lord is gracious will be hungry to feed themselves on the word of God.

If you do not study the word of God, this means you have not experienced the graciousness of God. "Gracious" comes from the word "grace." If you experience the grace of God that saved you, you will be hungry for the word of God, and you will open the Bible every day and read until you are filled and satisfied with His word. Thus, St. Peter is saying, "This is the proper practice for those who have tasted that the Lord is gracious, who have tasted the grace of God and converted to Christianity."

2:4 Coming to Him as to a living stone, rejected indeed by men, but chosen by God and precious. Come to Christ as if you are coming to a living stone. One of the many descriptions of Christ is that He is "the Stone," "the Rock," because He is the foundation upon whom we build our spiritual lives, and on whom we build the Church of God.

But He is not an empty stone; He is a "living stone." He is a living stone because He gives life to all who build their lives upon Him. If you build your spiritual life upon Christ, He will give you eternal life. The Lord Jesus Christ Himself lives eternally. He is the source of life. That is why He is the living stone.

rejected indeed by men. This refers to the Jews having rejected Him and crucified Him on the cross. They did not accept Him as the Messiah, as the Master, as the Lord and King; they rejected Him and crucified Him.

but chosen by God. God the Father chose His Son and made Him the King of kings and the Lord of lords. He is chosen by God the Father who also raised Him from the dead.

chosen by God and precious. The Lord Jesus Christ is precious in and of Himself. He is precious in the sight of the Father and He is also precious in our sight—in the sight of all believers.

St. Peter is saying: "When you believed and were baptized, you were born again and you came to Christ, you came to the living stone upon whom you will build your spiritual life. This stone was rejected by men, by the Jews, but you accepted Him because He is precious in your heart as He is precious in and of Himself. He is precious in the eyes of God the Father who raised Him from the dead and chose Him. So, while people rejected Him, the Father chose Him."

2:5 You also, as living stones, are being built up a spiritual house, a holy priesthood, to offer up spiritual sacrifices acceptable to God through Jesus Christ. If you build your life on the living stone, you will become a living stone. St. Peter is taking the metaphor of a building, and as this building has a foundation and there are stones built on this foundation; the Lord Jesus Christ is the stone, He is the foundation, but He is a living stone; so, those who build their lives on Him will also be living stones.

What does a "living stone" mean? It means that you will live eternally, as He lives eternally. When you are baptized, you take the promise of eternal life, and when you partake of His body and His blood, "He who eats My body and drinks My blood shall live forever" (cf. Jn 6:54); that is how we become living stones.

built up a spiritual house. We grow together to be the Church of God. Here, "the Church" has three meanings: (1) The first meaning is the building. (2) The second meaning is the assembly of the people. (3) The third meaning is the priests. Here, St. Peter is speaking about the second meaning, which is the assembly of the believers.

The Lord Jesus Christ is the foundation and we are the stones. Thus, all of us together make this building called, "the Church," but it is a spiritual house. Now, he is speaking about the spiritual house, and as the stones connect together, so are we united together with the bond of love. As the stones need each other to stand firm in their places, so we grow together, and we need each other in order to be strong in our spiritual lives.

The Lord Jesus Christ is the cornerstone because a cornerstone unites three dimensions together. As a cornerstone, He keeps me in peace with myself, He keeps me in peace with others, and He keeps me in peace with God. These are the three dimensions: with God, with others, and with oneself.

built up a spiritual house, a holy priesthood. When we speak about the priesthood, there are two types: (1) The sacramental priesthood. (2) The priesthood of the laity—of lay people. The sacramental priesthood is the ordained clergy, which was established by the Lord Jesus Christ Himself when

He appointed the twelve disciples, gave them the Holy Spirit, and gave them the authority to bind, to loose, and to forgive sins upon the earth (cf. Mt 18:18.) There is also what we call, "the priesthood of laity." Each one of you is considered a priest, not in the sacramental sense, but in the spiritual sense. What is the function of a priest? The priest's main function is to offer sacrifices. When you pray, you are offering a sacrifice of praise; in this sense you are a priest. When you help the poor, this is a sacrifice; in this sense you are a priest. Furthermore, the priest totally and fully consecrates his life to God. Thus, when you dedicate your life to Christ, in this sense, you are a priest.

St. Peter is saying, "Christ is the High Priest, and when we were baptized and anointed with the holy Myron Oil, all of us became spiritual priests, serving in the spiritual church; we became spiritual priests serving in the spiritual church. That is why he said, "a holy priesthood." "Holy" means dedicated to God, consecrated to God to offer up spiritual sacrifices, like the spiritual sacrifices of which St. Paul spoke in Hebrews 13:15 and in Romans 12:1, when he said, to "offer your body as a holy sacrifice to God." Also, the prophet David spoke about special sacrifices in Psalm 49:23 (Septuagint).

What are the spiritual sacrifices? They include praying, praising the Lord, good deeds, and consecrating your body and your life to the service of God. All these are considered spiritual sacrifices. In order to be acceptable to God the Father, you need to offer these sacrifices through Jesus Christ—in the name of the Lord Jesus Christ, because He is the way. Any humanitarian organization that helps the poor and those in need but not in the name of Christ, I cannot consider these as offering spiritual sacrifices. In order to offer spiritual sacrifices, they must be in the name of Christ. That is why St. Peter said, "to offer up spiritual sacrifices acceptable to God through Jesus Christ." Therefore, this must be done in the name of the Lord Jesus Christ.

2:6 **Therefore it is also contained in the Scripture, 'Behold, I lay in Zion A chief cornerstone, elect, precious, And he who believes on Him will by no means be put to shame.'** St. Peter is quoting a verse from Isaiah 28:16. That is why he said, "it is also contained," meaning it was mentioned in the Scripture: "Behold, I lay in Zion a chief cornerstone, elect, precious, and he who believes on Him will by no means be put to shame." St. Peter is saying: "The metaphor of the stone is actually not mine. I took it from the Scripture; I took it from Isaiah."

God told us through the prophecies that the Lord Jesus Christ is the living stone, the living foundation, and the cornerstone. If you read Isaiah 28, you will find that Isaiah spoke about this stone, that He is "a tried stone." A "tried stone" means He was tested and examined and proved to be a sure foundation. If you build upon Him, this building will not fall. He is "a tried stone, a precious cornerstone, a sure foundation." (Isaiah 28:16)

"Behold, I lay in Zion [in Jerusalem], a chief cornerstone (the main cornerstone, the main foundation), elect (because He was chosen by God the Father), precious (because He is the chief cornerstone without whom the structure, the whole Church, cannot be built)." The chief cornerstone is the main foundation. If you do not have the foundation, you cannot build anything. That is why He is precious.

"And he who believes on Him will by no means be put to shame." Of course, "believes on Him," means that this stone is not just a materialistic stone; he is referring to the Person of Jesus Christ, to the Person of the Messiah. "And he who believes in Him," is the basis of our salvation. If you believe in Him, you will not be ashamed. In the Day of Judgment, you will not be ashamed if you believed in Him, if you followed Him.

2:7 **Therefore, to you (the believers) who believe, He is precious; but to those who are disobedient (the unbelievers), 'The stone which the builders rejected has become the**

chief cornerstone.' "Therefore, to you who believe, He is precious; but to those who are disobedient [the unbelievers]," St. Peter is saying: "This prophecy is now fulfilled; the prophecy of Isaiah is now fulfilled. For us, the believers, He is precious because we were promised that if we believe in Him, we will not be ashamed in the Last Day."

St. Peter wanted to send a message to those who do not believe in Christ, and because of their unbelief, they disobey Him. He told them [the disobedient— the nonbelievers], "Hear what the Scripture said." He wants them to hear what the Scripture said, "The stone which the builders rejected has become the chief cornerstone."

Who are the builders? The religious leaders of Israel—they are the ones who crucified Him. They rejected Him instead of believing in Him. "The stone which the builders (the religious leaders) rejected has become the chief cornerstone." St. Peter is quoting Psalm 118:22, saying that now this stone that all the nation of Israel (especially the religious leaders) rejected, has become the head and the foundation of Christianity—of the Church of God.

instead of believing in Him; all the nonbelievers will stumble. So, He is to the disobedient a stone over which they stumble and fall. Therefore, instead of building your life on this sure foundation and becoming a living stone, if you do not believe in Him, you will stumble and fall upon this stone.

We see the difference between the Christians and the non-Christians. Christians build their lives upon Christ. Non-Christians blaspheme against Christ and they stumble and fall and commit many foolish deeds because they do not believe in Christ.

A stone of stumbling and a rock of offense. They stumble, being disobedient to the word (because they do not obey the word of God. That is why they stumble and fall), "to which they also were appointed." They were appointed to stumbling if they do not believe.

Thus, all the nonbelievers will stumble and fall. They will not be saved. They will not have eternal life. The unbelievers will stumble, fall, and perish forever because God has appointed from all eternity that he who does not believe in Him shall be condemned.

2:8 and 'A stone of stumbling And a rock of offense.' They stumble, being disobedient to the word, to which they also were appointed. This means that the Jews will stumble

2:9 But you are a chosen generation, a royal priesthood, a holy nation, His own special people, that you may proclaim the praises of

Him who called you out of darkness into His marvelous light. St. Peter now gives four beautiful descriptions of the Christian, saying:

But you are:

(1) **a chosen generation.** In the Old Testament, Israel was the chosen generation, the people of God, His chosen people. Now, we, the Christians, have become the chosen generation, an elect race. Now, we are His chosen people who believe in Him, who became the chosen people.

(2) **a royal priesthood.** St. Peter is quoting Exodus Chapter 19:6, but he replaced the term, "a kingdom of priests," with "a royal priesthood." When we are baptized, we do not only become spiritual priests, but we become the children of the King, and as children of the King, we, too, are kings—kings and queens. In this sense, our priesthood is a royal priesthood (royal versus the Levitical priesthood); it is a royal priesthood.

(3) **a holy nation.** This means we are set apart for God, we are sanctified by God, we are consecrated by God as a holy nation.

(4) **His own special people.** God became our Lord and we became His own special people. We became His own possession, different than the children of the world. Think about this privilege: We are His own special people. But, with this comes what? With all these privileges comes responsibility. What is the responsibility? St. Peter said, "That you may proclaim the praises of Him who called you out of darkness into His marvelous light."

Before knowing Christ, you were living in darkness, and now, Christ has called you from darkness into light. That is why you need to praise Him and to proclaim this praise in front of others, to witness to the Lord.

St. Paul said in his letter to the Ephesians, Chapter 2, "You are different from the children of the world." That is why you should shine by your good works. "For we are His workmanship, created in Christ Jesus for good works, which God prepared beforehand that we should walk in them" (Eph 2:10). Also, in the Sermon on the Mount, Jesus said, "Let your light so shine before men, that they may see your good works and glorify your Father in heaven" (Mt 5:16).

But here, St. Peter was speaking specifically about the Gentiles, the non-Jewish people, because in verse 10 he said, "you were not His people."

2:10 who once were not a people

but are now the people of God, who had not obtained mercy but now have obtained mercy. Israel, in the Old Testament, was called the people of God, but we, the Gentiles, were not called His people in the Old Testament. St. Peter is saying, "Before Christ you were not His people, but now, after Christ, you have become His people."

He is quoting Hosea 2:23. St. Peter quotes many of the prophets who spoke about the conversion of the Gentiles and how the Gentiles would join the Church of God and would become the people of God. Once you "were not a people but now the people of God."

who had not obtained mercy but now have obtained mercy. In the Old Testament, God was only dealing with the Jews and only had mercy on the Jews. In the Old Testament, the Gentiles did not enjoy the mercies of God, except a few exceptions like the Ninevites. But now, in the New Testament, all of us have obtained the mercies of God, and God saved all of us and allowed all of us who believe in Him to be His own special people.

2:11 Beloved, I beg you as sojourners and pilgrims abstain from fleshly lusts which war against the soul. St. Peter is telling them: "Now, you know who you are: you are a holy nation, a royal priesthood, a chosen generation, His own special

people. So, then, my beloved, knowing who you are, I want you to consider how you conduct yourselves in this world. I beg you as sojourners and pilgrims …"

"Sojourners" means that we are on a journey. While we are here on earth, we do not have an everlasting home. Our home is in heaven. Thus, we are on a journey toward heaven. If you understand that you are on a journey, if you understand that you are a pilgrim going to the holy place (the holy of the holies in heaven), what should you do? You should "abstain from fleshly lusts which war against the soul."

In your life, you will have desires of the flesh and desires of the spirit. Your spirit longs for God. Your flesh longs for sin. There is war between the desires of the flesh and the desires of the spirit. That is why he told them, "You are sojourners seeking your eternal home. You need to abstain from fleshly lusts, which would destroy your desire for that home. If you follow the fleshly lusts of the flesh, your eternal salvation will be at risk."

2:12 having your conduct honorable among the Gentiles, that when they speak against you as evildoers, they may, by your good works which they observe, glorify God in the day of visitation. St. Peter is saying, "The Gentiles among whom you were living are now accusing you with many charges. They are accusing you of being disobedient and rebellious. They are accusing you of atheism because you do not believe in their gods. There are many false accusations against you. Therefore, it is by your conduct, by your daily life, by your good works, that you will be able to refute those who slander you. How will you defend yourselves? Not by your words, but by your works."

That is why he said, "having your conduct honorable," because if your conduct is honorable, if your behavior is honorable among the Gentiles and the nonbelievers, even when they speak against you as evildoers, when they speak against you as being rebellious, when God visits them and they accept Christ (that is the day of visitation), they may glorify God.

The Gentiles and Jews often accused Christians of being rebellious, and because the Christians rejected the heathen gods, they were accused of being atheists. The best way to answer these charges is to prove the falsehood of their accusations by our Christian conduct. "Let your light so shine before men, that they may see your good works and glorify God who is in heaven" (Mt 5:16).

day of visitation. This refers to the day when God will clarify to them that He is the true Messiah, and they will believe in Him and convert to Christianity. That is the day of visitation, when the Gentiles and the non-believers believe in Christ, they will glorify God because of your good works.

It is like when we hear that a non-Christian became Christian; we ask how the Christians were dealing with him. In His testimony, he will say, "I was harsh with the Christians. I dealt with them with injustice and unfairness, but their behavior was totally different. They treated me in a different way." In this manner, they are glorifying God in the day of their visitation because of the good works of the Christians.

Now, the main accusation against them was that they were rebellious. That is why from verse 13, St. Peter is giving us some practical applications especially about being rebellious so that we do not rebel against authorities. That is why he said that to refute their accusations.

2:13 Therefore submit yourselves to every ordinance of man for the Lord's sake, whether to the king as supreme. St. Peter is saying, "Obey human laws because it is the Lord's will, but keep in mind, if the human law contradicts God's law, obey God. Other than this, you need to obey human laws, because this is the will of God for you to be obedient and submissive to authorities."

Furthermore, St. Peter gives us examples: "whether to the king as supreme" The Roman Emperor was called "supreme" in older provinces, to which this letter was addressed. Therefore, St. Peter is telling them, "The king is your supreme. That is why you need to submit yourself to the king."

2:14 **or to the governors, as to those who are sent by him (as if by God) for the punishment of evildoers and for the praise of those who do good.** The governors were placed over the provinces of the Roman Empire. Why do you need to submit to the governors? St. Peter is saying, "Rulers are necessary for the punishment of evildoers and for the praise of them that do well. That is why you need to submit to the governors. It is the governor's duty to punish the evildoers and to reward the good."

2:15 **For this is the will of God, that by doing good you may put to silence the ignorance of foolish men.** This is the will of God that you submit to the authorities. The foolish men who accuse us falsely, the foolish men who slander us, how will you put them to silence? Your good works is the best way to defend yourself. "This is the will of God, that by doing good you may put to silence the ignorance of foolish men" It is God's will that by your good works, you silence the

charges that are against you, which are that you are rebellious persons."

2:16 **as free, yet not using liberty as a cloak for vice, but as bondservants of God.** Christ has set us free. We are now free from the bondage of sin. We are not slaves to Satan. Now, we are free. Freedom does not mean irresponsibility and to live in chaos. That is why St. Peter said, "Yes, you are free, but do not use liberty as a cloak for vice. You say, 'Now I am free, I can do everything, even sin and vice.' Do not use your liberty as an excuse for wickedness, because you are now bondservants of God."

bondservants of God. St. Peter is referring to a tradition in the Old Testament where when a master had a slave, he was to set him free in the seventh year. But, if this slave in the seventh year said, "I love my master, he is kind to me, he is gracious to me, he is dear to me, and I want to continue in his service" (cf. Ex 5:21), now this servant is called a bondservant.

Furthermore, "bondservant" means that the slave is now attached and committed to serve his master by this bond. Which bond is this? It is the bond of love. Now, he is serving him [his master] out of love, not out of fear.

St. Peter is saying, "As bondservants of God, you choose to be His servants, and you are now bound to Him by His love. Because of this bond of love, you should not use your freedom and liberty as opportunity for vice."

2:17 Honor all people. Love the brotherhood. Fear God. Honor the king. St. Peter gave us four small commandments:

(1) **Honor all people:** This means to respect everybody regardless of who they are, regardless of their social status, regardless of their race or their color, whether they are rich or poor, Jews or Gentiles; honor all people.

(2) **Love the brotherhood:** Usually, the word, "brotherhood," means your brothers and sisters in Christ, the believers. Love the brotherhood as Christ loves us.

(3) **Fear God:** This means to respect Him, to walk in the fear of God, to revere Him. To revere God is not the type of fear of being petrified by Him. It is not like the fear of slaves, but rather, it is the respect and reverence of God.

(4) **Honor the king:** Honor, because the king is the servant of God. He is appointed by God to punish the evil and to reward the good.

Before we study verse 18, I want to explain something. Christianity does not encourage slavery. Some people use this passage to say that Christianity supports slavery. No, it does not at all. What St. Peter and St. Paul are saying is that if you are a slave (because there was slavery at that time), you should show your Christianity by your submission.

However, at the first opportunity to be set free, take this opportunity. They are not encouraging slavery or supporting it, but they are speaking to the Christians who are slaves as to what they should do. Therefore, he says to them in verse 18:

2:18 Servants, be submissive to your masters with all fear, not only to the good and gentle, but also to the harsh. So, here, when I submit to the harsh, I am submitting by my own will. I am not submitting out of fear. I am choosing to submit even to the harsh master to show my Christianity, to show the love of God in my heart. That is why St. Peter told them, "Servants, be submissive to your masters with all fear, with all respect, not only to the good and gentle, but also to the harsh."

The Greek word for "servants" means slaves. St. Peter is telling them to be submissive because it is their duty as servants or slaves, they must be submissive. Furthermore, true submission is not only to good masters, but also to the harsh masters, because I submit not out of fear of the master, but I submit because I fear God.

2:19 For this is commendable, if because of conscience toward God one endures grief, suffering wrongfully. "Commendable" means acceptable and praise worthy. Thus, he is saying that the conduct he described is acceptable before God. What does "endures grief, suffering wrongfully" mean? It means that if you suffer wrong for conscience sake toward God, that although you are doing good, you are punished and you accept this punishment, you accept the suffering not out of weakness, but you accept it out of your conscience toward God, because you want to fulfill the commandment of God.

If a man suffers for conscience sake, God will note his suffering and approve his conduct and praise him, commend him. It "is commendable, if because of conscience toward God one endures grief, suffering wrongfully."

2:20 For what credit is it if, when you are beaten for your faults, you take it patiently? But when you do good and suffer, if you take it patiently, this is commendable before God. St. Peter is saying, "If you

made a mistake and you are punished, and then you say, 'I am enduring this punishment because of God,' no, you are actually not; you are enduring the consequence of your behavior. You did something wrong, and that is the consequence. What credit is it if when you are beaten for your faults you take it patiently? To bear with patience punishment for faults is no glory."

But when you do good and suffer, if you take it patiently, this is commendable before God. What is really praiseworthy, what is really acceptable, what is really commendable before God, is when you patiently bear suffering inflicted for right doing. When you do something right, when you do something good, and are punished, but you accept and endure with patience, this punishment for God's sake is commendable before God.

2:21 For to this you were called, because Christ also suffered for us, leaving us an example, that you should follow His steps. St. Peter is saying, "For to this you were called." The Lord called us. We are told in the Gospel to enter through the narrow gate: "He who wants to be My disciple should carry his cross and follow Me" (cf. Mt 16:24). In fact, we are called to endure suffering. We are called to enter through the narrow gate. We should not consider it something strange when we suffer in the world. It is the experience of the Christian to suffer for right doing because it is to this that you were called. When you suffer because you did something right, you are following the example of the Lord Christ because "Christ also suffered for us, leaving us an example that we should follow His steps." Christ suffered although He did not do anything wrong, but He suffered and was crucified. He is our example.

2:22 Who committed no sin, nor was deceit found in His mouth. St. Peter is quoting Isaiah 53:9 and explaining to us that Christ did not do anything wrong to deserve suffering. The Lord Jesus Christ did not sin. They did not find any deceit or any mistake in His words. Jesus told them, "Who can rebuke Me or convict Me of sin?" (cf. John 8:46). Nobody was able to convict Him [the Lord Jesus]. Although Christ was sinless—completely sinless, verse 23 says:

2:23 who, when He was reviled, did not revile in return; when He suffered, He did not threaten, but committed Himself to Him who judges righteously. Do you see the example of Christ? When they reviled Him, He did not revile in return. When they made Him suffer, He did not threaten. He did not resent insults or suffering inflicted upon Him, but

what did He do? He submitted all the judgment to God. He committed Himself to God the Father who judges righteously. He gave the judgment between Him and His enemies over to God.

Thus, in the same way, let God avenge you, as according to St. Paul, "Do not avenge yourselves, because He said, 'Vengeance is mine, I will repay,' says the Lord" (cf. Deut 32:35; Rom 12:19). We need to follow His example; for it was by doing this (accepting suffering) that He was going to save us. By His suffering on the cross, we are saved. That is why in verse 24 St. Peter said:

2:24 who Himself bore our sins in His own body on the tree, that we, having died to sins, might live for righteousness—by whose stripes you were healed. He died for our sins, not for His sins, because He is sinless; He is the Holy One. He suffered not for doing wrong, but for doing right. He died for our sins. He took our burdens in His body. He is the Lamb of God who took away the sins of the whole world on the tree, which means on the cross.

who Himself bore our sins in His own body on the tree, that we, having died to sins. In baptism, we actually die to sin. In baptism, you are crucified with Him. Therefore, in baptism, we are baptized into His death, then we rise with Him into a new life, and now we live in righteousness. That is why we dress the newly baptized in white after their baptism as a symbol of righteousness.

Thus, St. Peter says, He "who Himself bore our sins in His own body on the tree, that we, having died to sins (in baptism), might live for righteousness" Now, we should live a righteous and godly life because He purified us; He cleansed us. Our lives should now be righteous and pure.

By whose stripes you were healed. His suffering led to our salvation, and our healing. By His sufferings, we were saved. By His stripes we were healed. St. Peter is quoting Isaiah 53:5-6.

2:25 For you were like sheep going astray, but have now returned to the Shepherd and Overseer of your souls. St. Peter is saying, "Before Christ, we were lost sheep, we were prodigal children. You were like sheep going astray, led astray by sin and the pleasures of the world. But now, having now returned by the coming of Christ, by His salvation, by His crucifixion and His suffering, now you have returned to the Shepherd and Overseer of your souls."

St. Peter is giving two descriptions of Christ: "Shepherd" and "Overseer." Shepherd, because we are His sheep. He is a good Shepherd who died for the sheep; the good Shepherd gives up his life for the sheep.

The word, "overseer" in Greek, "episcopos," means one who leans over, scopes, like a microscope or a telescope. It means to see. Episcopos means overseer. The word, "bishop," in Greek is also episcopos, because a bishop oversees all the churches and the needs of his flock.

Now, St. Peter is saying, "The Lord Jesus Christ is your Shepherd and your Bishop, your Overseer who watches over His flock and cares for them." That is why he also said in Chapter 3:12, "The eyes of the Lord are over the righteous." His eyes are over us, overseeing us. He gives us His Spirit and feeds and guides us by His words. He is our Shepherd and the Overseer of our souls.

~~~~~~~~~~

Chapter 2 Questions

1. What must we lay aside to grow spiritually?

2. How should we long for the word if we want to grow spiritually?

3. What should motivate us to desire the word with such longing?

4. What kind of stone is used to describe Jesus?

5. What is Jesus to those who believe in Him and to those who do not believe?

6. What is the appointed end of those who do not believe and are disobedient?

7. How are Christians described by St. Peter? What is their duty? Why?

8. What is our duty as sojourners and pilgrims in this world? Why?

9. What is our duty toward the governments of men? Why?

10. How are we to use our freedom in Christ?

11. What four admonitions summarize our duties to others?

12. What is the duty of servants to their masters?

13. What is commendable before God?

14. To what have we been called?

15. How did Jesus suffer wrongly and bear it patiently?

16. What good did Jesus accomplish by suffering such abuse (24-25)?

3

Chapter Outline

• Submission to husands(1-6)
• A word to husbands (7)
• Called to blessing (8-12)
• Suffering for right and wrong (13-17)
• Christ's suffering and ours (18-22)

Introduction

St. Peter continues to describe the duties of Christian living and how to live a Christian life, especially when we know that we are sojourners and pilgrims in this world, that we do not have a permanent city here, but we are on a journey toward eternal life.

He starts this chapter by counseling the wives to be submissive to their own husbands, and to also focus their adornment not on outward appearances, but on the development of a meek and quiet and gentle spirit. After he instructed the wives, he also instructed the husbands to live with their wives in an understanding way, by honoring them, because they will receive an equal honor in eternity, and by understanding their nature as the weaker (more fragile) vessel and as fellow heirs of the grace of life.

After he addresses the relationship between husbands and wives, he addresses the relationship with our brethren. "Our brethren," means our fellow Christians. He was emphasizing unity, compassion, love, kindness, and courtesy. Then, he told us, "If you are mistreated by your brother, the proper response is to respond with a blessing. If your brother reviled you, you bless him. This is the way to be blessed in your life. If you want to have a good life, to enjoy a happy life, the key point is to turn away from evil and to do good, to seek peace, to be a peacemaker, and to pursue it" (cf. 1 Pet 3:8-12).

St. Peter concludes the chapter by addressing the issue of suffering, especially at that time when many Christians were suffering because of their religion and for the sake of righteousness. He tells them, "In order to prepare yourselves for suffering, you should sanctify the Lord in your hearts, and you should live a godly life (cf. 1 Pet 3:15). That is how to prepare for suffering. And not only that, but you also need to be ready to give a reason for your hope, a reason why you are Christian and why you endure suffering, pain, and hardships for Christ's sake. When you give this response, you need to give it in meekness and humbleness, not in arrogance."

To appreciate our suffering for righteousness's sake, that it can be for good, St. Peter gives us the example of our Lord Jesus Christ who suffered for our sins, although He is the Holy One, separated from sins. St. Peter also explains how Christ died on the cross and descended to Hades and preached (i.e., announced) the good news of salvation of His opening the doors of Paradise, to all souls (the righteous, as well as to the disobedient; the disobedient, blinded by darkness did not accept Christ's preaching, but the righeous rejoiced and were taken to Paradise).

He then draws a comparison between Noah's ark and baptism, saying, "As the people were saved through the ark of Noah, through the water, now we are saved through baptism. And baptism is not to wash our bodies, but it is an appeal for the good conscience. And the power of baptism comes from the resurrection of Christ, because baptism is burial and resurrection with Christ" (1 Pet 3:18-22).

3:1 Wives, likewise, be submissive to your own husbands, that even if some do not obey the word, they, without a word, may be won by the conduct of their wives. In the early centuries, in the 1st Century, many individuals converted to Christianity while their spouses had not converted to Christianity, so we had many families or many couples in which one person was Christian, but the other was not. In St. Paul's First Epistle to the Corinthians,

he told them, "You should not separate nor divorce. If the unbeliever wants to leave, let him leave, but if the unbeliever wants to stay, then you should not leave him. You should not leave him" (cf. 1 Cor 7:10-16).

St. Peter is now addressing whether wives should submit to their husbands even if he is an unbeliever. When we speak about submission here, it is the submission of love. We read in 1 Corinthians 15:28, "Now when all things are made subject to Him, then the Son Himself will also be subject to Him who put all things under Him, that God may be all in all. This submission is a submission of love. It is like when the Son, our Lord Jesus Christ, prayed in Gethsemane and said, "Father, let it be according to Your will and not according to My will" (cf. Mt 26:39; Luke 22:42).

Christianity teaches that the wife should show obedience and submission to her husband. If he is Christian, she should definitely submit to him and obey him, but there was a question: What about the nonbelievers? What about those who do not obey the Lord, the word of the Lord? Thus, St. Peter answered and said, "Wives, likewise, be submissive to your own husbands," and he used the word "own" to indicate that it is right to submit to them.

That even if some do not obey the word, they, without a word, may be won by the conduct of their

wives. He is saying, "Your unbelieving husband, when he sees your Christian conduct, your obedience, your respect, your submission, you will win him to Christ, even without preaching a word."

Therefore, the wife should show obedience and submission that she may win her husband. Unbelievers may be quietly won by the Christian lives of their wives. Furthermore, St. Peter also emphasized conduct, not only submission, but the whole conduct and behavior of the wife, when he said in verse 2:

3:2 when they observe your chaste conduct accompanied by fear. St. Paul is saying, "When your husband sees and observes your pure and chaste conduct, that you are walking in the fear of God, this in itself can lead him to Christ." In addition, he is also saying that if the husband is Christian, but he does not obey the word of God, which means he is living an ungodly life, by the submission and obedience of his wife, by her pure and chaste conduct, she will be able to win her husband to Christ. The word "fear" may refer to both the fear of God as well as respect to the husband.

While St. Peter was urging this pure and holy life, he also wanted to address a bad habit in which some women may do, which is focusing on outward adornment while neglecting adorning

their souls and their spirits. That is why St. Peter says:

3:3 Do not let your adornment be merely outward- arranging the hair, wearing gold, or putting on fine apparel. Do not focus on outward adornment. St. Peter is condemning the unrestrained indulgence and exhibits of some women. The important part is to keep your heart adorned with the virtues and the fruit of the Holy Spirit. What will it profit you if your outer appearance is beautiful, but from within, you do not look beautiful? That is why St. Peter is saying, "The important part here is to keep your heart right and your spirit adorned with the graces and the fruits and the virtues of the Holy Spirit." That is why in verse 4 he says:

3:4 rather let it be the hidden person of the heart, with the incorruptible beauty of a gentle and quiet spirit, which is very precious in the sight of God. Here, he is making a comparison between outward beauty and inward beauty. He is saying, "The outward beauty is clear to everybody, anybody can see it, but the inward beauty is mainly seen by God."

Yes, others can also observe the purity

and chastity of my heart, but who will know everything about my heart? It is only God. That is why St. Peter says, "the hidden person of the heart." The external beauty will be corrupted one day, either with old age or with death, but the internal beauty is incorruptible; nothing can corrupt the beauty of the heart.

St. Peter focused on one virtue here: the virtue of gentleness and a quiet spirit—quietness and gentleness. I think he chose this virtue because it goes hand in hand with submission. A submissive wife will be gentle, kind, quiet, calm. She will not scream and yell and argue. That is why St. Peter is saying, "You need to seek the incorruptible adorning of gentleness and quietness rather than the outward adornment."

Furthermore, he says, "When God sees your heart as a gentle and quiet heart, this is very, very precious in His sight. Such adorning is of great worth in the sight of God." St. Peter gives us an example from the holy women in the Scripture, taking the example of Sarah. Why did he use Sarah as an example? He is saying that since Abraham is the father of the Jews and Gentiles (the Jews are his children by flesh, but the Gentiles are his children by faith), so if Abraham is our father, then Sarah is our mother, and so we need to learn from our mother. That is why he told them:

3:5 For in this manner, in former times, the holy women who trusted in God also adorned themselves, being submissive to their own husbands. How did these holy women like Sarah adorn themselves? By being submissive to their husbands, by being gentle and quiet with their husbands; that is how Sarah adorned herself.

However, usually with submission comes fear. What if the other person is taking advantage of me? What if the other person starts to abuse me because I chose to submit to him? That is why St. Peter said, "Who trusted in God," because when you choose to submit, you choose to submit not out of fear like the slaves, but you choose to submit because it is the commandment of God, and you trust God.

God will defend you as he defended Sarah when she wanted to protect her son Isaac from Ishmael (seeking to cast out Ishmael and his mother Hagar). Abraham was displeased with this idea, but God defended Sarah and said to Abraham, "Whatever Sarah says to you, do it wholeheartedly" (cf. Gen 21:12).

Therefore, if you trust God and choose to submit, God will protect you from being exploited or abused. Holy women trust in God, and submit to Him, because they trust in Him, not because of fear—"the holy women who trusted in God also adorned themselves, being submissive to their own husbands."

3:6 **as Sarah obeyed Abraham, calling him lord, whose daughters you are if you do good and are not afraid with any terror.** Sarah, in her obedience and submission, addressed Abraham by calling him, "lord," or "master." Also, in 1 Samuel 1:15, we read that Hannah, the mother of Samuel, addressed her husband in the same way. In the Orthodox Crowning Ceremony, during the commandments spoken to the bride, we read these verses from 1 Peter 3. However, some people do not like this passage or they take it as being funny, and so they do not take it seriously, although it is part of the Scripture.

Some people have dared to change this in the text of the Crowning Ceremony, and to change it to something they think is more acceptable, as if they need to discuss it together before they decide. This is not the commandment. The commandment is very clear and is part of the Scripture.

whose daughters you are. Now, he is saying that as Abraham is our father, Sarah is our mother, and if you want to be her daughters, you need to do as she has done. Thus, women should follow Sarah's example because she is the mother Abraham's children.

if you do good and are not afraid with any terror. What would make a wife afraid? She would be afraid if she does not do well. Thus, fear, here, might result from not doing well, but it may also come from lack of faith, because as was just explained, one may be afraid of being exploited or of being abused.

However, St. Peter is saying, "You should not be afraid with any terror because you do this because you trust in God and God will defend you." That is why if you are a quiet and submissive, loving wife, and you follow God's commandments, God will defend you.

This obedience and submission are in Christ—in God. What do I mean by this? If the unbelieving husband or the ungodly husband instructed his wife to do something against Christianity, against the commandment of God, then, with respect and with humbleness, she should refuse without being afraid of any terror. This submission does not mean that wives will be kept from the Christian commandments or Christian duties because of fear of threats. No, but by humbleness and meekness and gentleness, they will refuse to do anything against the commandment of God, even if they were threatened to do it.

After St. Peter addressed the wives, he addressed the husbands.

3:7 **Husbands, likewise, dwell with them with understanding, giving honor to the wife, as to the weaker vessel, and as being heirs together of the grace of life, that your prayers**

may not be hindered. "Dwell with them" means do not divorce them, do not abandon them, because "what God joined together, no man shall separate" (cf. Mk 10:9).

Dwell with them with understanding. St. Peter is instructing the husband to have knowledge about his wife. What knowledge? (1) St. Peter described women as being the "weaker vessel," and weaker vessel here means that they are fragile. When you carry something fragile, you carry it with caution; otherwise, it will break. St. Peter is saying, "You should know the nature of your wife; she is fragile. Because of the emotional nature of women, men ought to be more understanding. That is why they (men) need to dwell with them (women) with understanding by understand their gentle and sensitive nature."

Furthermore, do not consider them inferior to you just because God instructed them to submit to you. This does not mean you are superior to them and they are inferior to you. St. Peter says, "No. I want you to know that they are heirs together with you of the grace of life. They will inherit the kingdom of God. They will inherit eternal life as equal to you. Therefore, if God treated them as equals, you should not treat them as inferior or less than you. You need to build your house based on this knowledge."

giving honor to the wife. The wife was asked or is asked to submit to her husband, and the husband is asked or instructed to give honor to his wife— to give her honor, to put her in front of himself, to put her needs in front of his own needs. As St. Paul said in Romans 12:10, "Giving honor to them before yourselves," St. Peter is giving the same meaning here: "Giving honor to the wife, as to the weaker vessel, and as being heirs together of the grace of life."

Then, St. Peter said something very, very serious. He said, "that your prayers may not be hindered," which means that if the husband does not treat his wife with honor, if the husband does not treat his wife as an equal, if the husband is not considerate of the fragility of his wife ("the weaker vessel"), understanding her nature, when he prays, God will not accept his prayers. That is why St. Peter said, "That your prayers may not be hindered." Therefore, how you are treating your wife is an important factor in God's acceptance of your prayers.

In addition, St. Peter is saying, "The mutual prayers that you pray for her and she prays for you will be difficult if there is no mutual love and no mutual understanding." That is why St. Peter told the husband to treat his wife with honor, knowing that she is the weaker vessel, and that she will inherit the grace of life as equal to him; otherwise, his prayers will be hindered.

From verse 8, St. Peter starts to address

how to treat one another as brothers and sisters in Christ.

3:8 **finally, all of you be of one mind, having compassion for one another; love as brothers, be tenderhearted, be courteous.** St. Peter gives us five important commandments for Christian living:

(1) **all of you be of one mind:** To be of one mind, though we may disagree, the disagreement will never break our unity and our oneness because all of us have one goal, which is our salvation and the inheritance of the kingdom of God. When a house is divided against itself, it will be destroyed. When the Church is divided against itself, it will be destroyed. When any kingdom or nation is divided against itself, it will be destroyed. That is why he said, "finally, all of you be of one mind."

(2) **having compassion for one another:** God wants us to be merciful, compassionate in our heart, to have a delicate heart like in the parable of the good Samaritan. Unfortunately, the priest and the Levite did not have compassion for this Jewish person who was attacked by robbers. It was only the Samaritan who had compassion on him. Thus, St. Peter is telling us,

"You, as Christians, should have compassion for each other and should feel for one another."

(3) **love as brothers:** This is a sign of our discipleship to Christ. The Lord Jesus Christ told us, "By this all will know that you are My disciples, if you have love for one another" (cf. Jn 13:35).

(4) **be tenderhearted:** If there is a tender part in your body, when you touch it, you will feel pain. To be tenderhearted means you need to feel the pain of others. Suffer with others, weep with others, and rejoice with others. This is tenderheartedness. "Rejoice with those who rejoice, and weep with those who weep" (Rom 12:15).

(5) **be courteous:** Courtesy is a picture of love and respect—love and respect. We need to deal with one another with honor, with respect, with courtesy.

What if somebody mistreated me? What if somebody reviled me? What should I do? St. Peter tells us in verse 9.

3:9 **not returning evil for evil or reviling for reviling, but on the contrary blessing, knowing that you were called to this, that you may inherit a blessing.** He is telling us that if somebody does me evil, I should repay his evil with good. I should not repay evil with evil, but I repay evil with good. If somebody reviled me, as a Christian, I should repay him with a blessing, I should not return evil for evil or reviling for reviling.

God told us to bless others. Why? Even when they revile us, this is the way to be blessed. St. Peter tells us: "You were called to this, that you may inherit a blessing." Do you want to have blessing in your life? Do you want Christ to bless you in everything you do? Do not ever return evil for evil or reviling for reviling, but you need to bless, because as we read in Galatians 6:7, "whatever a man sows, that he will also reap." Therefore, if you sow blessing, you will reap blessing, but if you sow reviling and cursing, that also you will reap.

In verse 10, St. Peter quotes some verses from the Book of Psalms: Psalm 34:13-17. This is how the Psalm reads:

3:10 **For 'He who would love life and see good days, let him refrain his tongue from evil, and his lips from speaking deceit.'** In Psalm 34, our teacher David is giving us direction on how to live a good life. If you want to live a happy life, if you want to see good days, if you want to inherit a blessing, you need to abstain from evil, you need to refrain your tongue from evil, you need to refrain your lips from

deceiving others. The opposite is also true. Those who are not refraining their tongues from evil and deceive others, they will not see good days in their lives, and they will not see a happy and good life.

3:11 **'Let him turn away from evil and do good; let him seek peace and pursue it.'** He is saying, "Abstain from evil, and do good to everybody, even to those who curse you, to those who persecute you, to those who revile you. Do good to them and live peacefully with everybody."

He uses a very nice verb here when he says, "let him seek peace and pursue it." To pursue it means that even if peace seems like it is escaping from you, fleeing from you, you need to pursue it, to be a peacemaker, to pursue and seek peace with everybody. This is how Christians should live with one another.

3:12 **'For the eyes of the Lord are on the righteous, and His ears are open to their prayers; But the face of the Lord is against those who do evil.'** Do you remember when St. Peter said to the husbands, "lest your prayers be hindered?" (cf. 1 Pet 3:7). He is now telling us how God will hear our prayers. He is saying, "If you live a righteous life, if you refrain from evil words, if you abstain from evil deeds, God's eyes will observe you, will regard you, will see you, and His ears will be listening to your prayers. Whatever you pray, God will hear your prayer and He will answer your prayer, 'For the eyes of the Lord are on the righteous, and His ears are open to their prayers.'"

But the face of the Lord is against those who do evil. This is a very difficult verse. Who can stand against God? If I do evil, God will be against me. Who can endure this? Who can take this? Therefore, it is either to repay evil for evil and have God be against you, or to repay evil with blessing and to have God be with you and listening to your prayers. God is not pleased with evildoers. God turns away His pleasure from evildoers.

But again, when we hear, "turn the other cheek, let peace be, do not repay evil with evil," we usually feel insecure. This lack of faith makes us worried about others taking advantage of us or hurting us, but St. Peter is telling us, "Nobody can hurt you unless this is the will of God, unless it is with God's permission; only if God gave them permission."

I remember the story of David and King Saul (cf. 1 Samuel). When King Saul wanted to kill David, David told him, "Listen, if God did not allow you to kill me, you will never be able to kill me, and if God gave you permission to kill me, you will kill me. My life is not in your hands. My life is in the hand of God." David never repaid the evil of King Saul with evil. Rather, David repaid Saul's evil with goodness. That is why King Saul told him, "You are more righteous than I; for you have rewarded me with good, whereas I have rewarded you with evil. (1 Sam 24:17)."

That is why St. Peter tells us:

3:13 And who is he who will harm you if you become followers of what is good? Do not be afraid. Do not be afraid that people will take advantage of you. Do not be afraid that people will hurt you or harm you. Do not be afraid that people will abuse you if you do not repay evil with evil and if you do not repay reviling with reviling. Nobody can harm you. Nobody can hurt you unless it is by the permission of God and for your own benefit, for your own spiritual profit, as St. Peter will explain in the rest of the chapter.

Thus, he is saying, "If you are zealous for good, nobody can hurt you, nobody can harm you, nobody can abuse you or take advantage of you, because the eyes of God are upon you and His ears listen to your prayers. Who can be against you? Nobody can be against you."

3:14 But even if you should

suffer for righteousness' sake, you are blessed. And do not be afraid of their threats, nor be troubled. You are blessed if God allowed you to suffer for the sake of righteousness. Suffering is the way of glory. Suffering is the way of blessing. If it is God's will for you to suffer for the sake of righteousness, it is because He wants to give you a blessing. "Blessed are you when they revile and persecute you, and say all kinds of evil against you falsely for My sake. Rejoice and be exceedingly glad, for great is your reward in heaven," (Mt 5:11-12).

God may allow me to suffer for righteousness' sake, but why would He allow this? He would do this to give me a blessing, and to give me a great reward. You may be called to suffer for Christ, but instead of calling this evil, instead of you considering it evil and complaining about suffering for righteousness' sake, St. Peter is saying, "Blessed are you, happy are you, for great is your reward in heaven." The Psalm also says, "Those who sow in tears, shall reap in joy" (Ps 126:5). Thus, when we sow in tears, we will reap in joy.

St. Peter continued to say in verse 14, "And do not be afraid of their threats, nor be troubled." When wicked people threaten you, do not be afraid, and do not be troubled, because your life is not in the hands of people, but in the hand of God.

These days, many people are concerned about what is going on in Egypt and the threats of fanatical Muslims. The message for us is very clear. "Do not be afraid of their threats nor be troubled," because who can harm you? Nobody can harm you; nobody can hurt you. If God allowed you to suffer for righteousness' sake, happy are you, blessed are you, for your reward is great in heaven.

How can I deal with this suffering or this persecution? How will I be ready for this blessing? "Blessed are you when they persecute you," (Mt 5:11). He tells us how in verse 15.

3:15 But sanctify the Lord God in your hearts, And always be ready to give a defense to everyone who asks you a reason for the hope that is in you, with meekness and fear. Let God be sanctified in your heart. Let Him be honored in your heart. How do we sanctify God in our hearts? It is as we say in the Lord's Prayer, "Hallowed be Thy Name" (Mt 6:9). How do we sanctify God? It is by living a godly life, by living a holy life, by obeying the commandment of God, by making my heart a resting place for Christ so that Christ can look at my heart and say, "This is the place for My rest. I will dwell here; I will rest in this heart." "Sanctify the Lord God in your hearts."

And not only that, St. Peter also says, "And always be ready to give a defense to everyone who asks you a reason for the hope that is in you." Besides sanctifying the Lord God in your heart, you need to be ready. Those who will persecute you will ask you why are you Christian, and why do you prefer to suffer rather than to deny your faith and convert to another religion. Here, you need to be ready. Always be ready to give a defense, to give a reason for the hope that is in you. Instead of fearing them, we need to be ready to confess Christ as the reason of our hope.

From St. George's biography, we see how he was able to give a defense to explain the reason for his hope in Christ. They persecuted him and he suffered for seven years, but he did not deny Christ. Because Christ is the reason of our hope, whoever follows Christ will be glorified in heaven, and whoever denies Christ will be denied. That is why St. Peter is telling us to be ready to explain to others the reason for our hope, which is Christ; the resurrected Christ who promised us the eternal life.

Give a defense to everyone who asks you a reason for the hope that is in you, with meekness and fear. When you answer and explain the reason of your hope, do not do this with arrogance. Do not do this with indignation and wrath, but do it with meekness, with fear, and with respect. St. Peter is teaching us how to even respect those who persecute us, and when we respond to them, we are to respond with respect, with reverence, and with meekness.

Unfortunately, many people who try to defend Christianity and defend the rights of Copts, do not follow St. Peter's instructions and they present a very, very bad image of Christians and Coptic Christians. That is why St. Peter is telling us, "When you give the defense, when you give the reason for your hope, do it with meekness and fear;" "Fear," here, means respect, reverence.

3:16 **having a good conscience, that when they defame you as evildoers, those who revile your good conduct in Christ may be ashamed.** He tells us, "You need to have a good conscience. You need to sanctify the Lord, because if you are not living a godly life, they [persecutors] will have a reason to defame you; but, if you are living a godly life and they defame you, they will be put to shame because they will not find anything against you, to defame you as evildoers."

Having a good conscience before God is an element of strength when we are accused. When we are persecuted, it is an element of strength to have a good conscience before God. Those who accuse us falsely or those who persecute us will be ashamed because they will not find any reason. They will not find any reason to defame us because we have a good conscience and good behavior in Christ. Thus, we can say that a holy life and a pure life are the best answer to the false accusers.

3:17 For it is better, if it is the will of God, to suffer for doing good than for doing evil. Now, he is comparing a person who did evil and is suffering because of the evil that he has done, with another person who did no evil but is suffering for righteousness' sake. St. Peter is asking, "Which is better?" If you suffer from evil, you are reaping what you sowed, but if you suffer while you are doing good, you are suffering for Christ's sake, and blessed are you; "your reward is great in heaven" (Lk 6:23; cf. 5:12).

Furthermore, he says, "if it is the will of God," meaning that God may allow us to suffer to give us a blessing, to discipline us, to chasten us. And we who honor the will of God will be comforted to know that this suffering is because of God's will, not because we did something wrong. It is better to suffer for well doing than for evil doing, for righteousness than for evil.

To encourage us, St. Peter gave us the example of the Lord Jesus Christ Himself who is the Holy One, separated from sinners, who never did any evil. Not only that, but He cannot do anything evil because He is God, the All Holy, the Holy One; yet, despite this, our Lord Jesus Christ suffered.

3:18 For Christ also suffered once for sins, the just for the unjust, that He might bring us to God, being put to death in the flesh but made alive by the Spirit. He said that Christ also suffered. The Holy One, He suffered. He is our example. He suffered for us. He said, "once." Once is referring to the one Sacrifice that Jesus offered Himself one time, unlike the high priests of the Jewish nation who offer sacrifices every year and every day. St. Peter is saying that Christ offered Himself once for all, only once.

But why did He suffer? He did not suffer because He did something wrong; He was just, but He suffered for the unjust, for us. He suffered in order to bring us back to God, to reconcile us back to God, to save us. So, we are the sinners and He took our sin in His body. We are the ones who transgressed the commandment of God and He accepted to die on the cross and to suffer for us.

St. Paul said, "It is very difficult for somebody to accept to suffer for a righteous man (cf. Rom 5:7), but Christ did not suffer for righteous people." He suffered for the ungodly, for transgressors, for the unjust. He suffered not for the good, but for those who have transgressed the commandments of God. He suffered to bring us to the graces of God and to reconcile us with God.

being put to death in the flesh. By the wounds inflicted in His fleshly body,

He died. His natural earthly body died on the cross. He died, "but made alive by the Spirit," because on the third day, He rose from the dead by the power of His divinity, by the Holy Spirit, and by the Father. "Made alive by the Spirit," He returned to life; He rose from the dead on the third day.

Then, we come to verse 19, which is one of the most difficult verses in the Scripture; so, let us try to understand it together.

3:19 by whom also He went and preached to the spirits in prison. "By whom" is referring to the Spirit. St. Peter is saying that Jesus Christ, by His Spirit … because after His death, what happened? His human soul was separated from His human body. His human spirit was separated from His human body. But His divinity was still united to His human spirit and His human body, and with this human spirit, He descended into Hades ("prison" here is referring to Hades). Thus, after Christ died, He went to Hades. The Greek word for "prison" means "a place of custody," not a place of punishment; thus, this refers to Hades, the wicked place.

I say this was difficult. Why? It is because of the word "preached." Preached, here, means announced. What did He announce? He announced that the doors of Paradise were open,

and now all the righteous people who were in Hades went with Christ to the Paradise of Joy. He opened the door of Paradise and took all the righteous people who died in the hope of the resurrection, who were in Hades, and took them into Paradise. In verse 20, St. Peter said that Christ not only preached to the righteous, but that He also preached to the disobedient.

3:20 who formerly were disobedient, when once the Divine long-suffering waited in the days of Noah, while the ark was being prepared, in which a few, that is, eight souls, were saved through water. St. Peter is saying, "God in the Spirit, the Lord Jesus Christ in the Spirit, went and preached not only for the godly people, but also for those who were disobedient and were in prison."

But what is the purpose of preaching to the disobedient? All the Church Fathers, when they interpreted this verse said that although He preached to them the resurrection, the salvation, and the opening of the door of Paradise, they were blind; they did not accept it. That is why only the righteous people rejoiced at the resurrection of Christ, rejoiced at the opening of the doors of Paradise, and only the righteous people went with Him to Paradise.

Thus, preaching was not for everybody, but the souls that were living in darkness of sin during their lives here on earth, they were also in darkness in Hades, and that is why they could not see, they could not hear, and they could not accept the preaching of Christ.

St. Peter is giving us the similar example of Noah by saying that as he preached to the people and asked them to enter with him into the ark, they refused and did not enter the ark (only eight persons entered the ark). In the same way, in Hades, they refused to accept the preaching of Christ. That is why he said, "who formerly were disobedient, when once the Divine long-suffering waited in the days of Noah, while the ark was being prepared."

The ark was built in 120 years; and for 120 years God waited. "Waited" means that He did not flood the world, hoping that these people would accept the preaching of Noah and enter the ark to be saved. But these people refused to accept the preaching of Noah and refused to enter the ark. God's long-suffering waited for 120 years while the ark was being prepared, but unfortunately, they refused to obey the call for repentance and only eight persons—Noah and his wife, their three sons and their wives. These were the eight persons out of the great multitude that were saved.

The number eight is the number of the resurrection. If Christ entered and was crucified on the sixth day, Friday, then, the day of the resurrection is the eighth

day.

Eight persons were saved in Noah's ark, and in the Bible, there are eight miracles regarding the resurrection: Elijah raised one person, Elisha, his disciple, raised two persons, the Lord Jesus Christ raised three persons, St. Peter raised one person, and St. Paul raised one person—eight persons in total.

God created the world in six days, and we are now living in the seventh day. The eighth day will be the day of the general resurrection (cf. Jn 5:28–29; Dan 12:2).

Thus, the number eight is the number for the resurrection. Baptism is the burial and resurrection of Christ. That is why when you visit old churches you see that when they built the baptismal font, they built it octagonal, with eight angles, because eight is the symbol of resurrection.

Furthermore, he said that eight persons "were saved through water." Now, St. Peter wants to link Noah's ark with baptism. Therefore, he says that these people were saved through water because the water was carrying the ark and eight persons were saved. The word, "symbol," means type, and the fulfillment of a symbol is called the "antitype." If we say that the ark is a type, then, the antitype is baptism. If we say that "manna" is a type, then, the antitype will be "Communion." If we say the "Passover Lamb" is a type, then, the antitype is "Christ," our Passover Lamb.

3:21 **There is also an antitype which now saves us—baptism (not the removal of the filth of the flesh, but the answer of a good conscience toward God), through the resurrection of Jesus Christ.**

antitype. This means the fulfillment of the symbol; the fulfillment of the symbol of the ark of Noah.

which now saves us—baptism. This is very clear. Protestants argue that you are not saved by baptism, but, here, St. Peter is saying it very clearly that, "There is also an antitype which now saves us—baptism." The Holy Gospel according to St. Mark 16:16 says, "He who believes and is baptized will be saved." Therefore, baptism is essential for salvation. Thus, now the antitype (baptism) saves us, as the water saved them by carrying them up in the ark; now, the water of baptism will save us.

St. Peter is comparing between the purification in the Jewish tradition and in baptism. Purification in the Jewish tradition was like removing the filth of the flesh. Thus, he said:

not the removal of the filth of the flesh, but the answer of a good conscience toward God. He is saying that baptism is not like the Jewish ceremonial washing which was only the purification of the flesh, but it is the answer of a good conscience.

the answer of a good conscience. Do you remember on the day of the Pentecost when the people asked Peter, "What should we do?" St. Peter told them to repent and be baptized. Therefore, baptism is the answer to those who are seeking a good conscience, because in baptism, we are born again; the old man is buried, and we are born again with a new nature. Thus, in baptism, we receive the good conscience, we receive the new man, and we receive the pure conscience that is the answer of a good conscience.

If you are asking, "What should I do?" and you are not Christian and you are not baptized, I will tell you to repent and be baptized. To the soul that is seeking forgiveness of sin and inquires, "What shall I do to remove the unforgiven sins and to make my conscience void of offense?" The answer is to repent and be baptized. He who obeys the word of God has the answer to this question in baptism.

but the answer of a good conscience toward God, through the resurrection of Jesus Christ. Baptism would be meaningless, would have no power and no effect, if Christ did not rise from the dead. The power of baptism comes from the resurrection of Christ. We are buried with Him in baptism and we are raised with Him in baptism. This burial and resurrection are with the Lord, as we read in Romans 6:1-6.

Forty days after His resurrection, the Lord, Jesus ascended to heaven and was glorified and honored. In the same way, after we are resurrected with Him in baptism, we will go to heaven and we will be honored with Him.

3:22 **who has gone into heaven and is at the right hand of God, angels and authorities and powers having been made subject to Him.** So as Christ's exaltation followed His death and resurrection, in the same way, our exaltation will follow our death with Christ and our resurrection with Him in baptism. St. Peter is saying that Christ endured suffering, and although He is righteous, He voluntarily endured suffering to set an example for us.

If we accept suffering and persecution for Christ's sake, as He is exalted now, we will be exalted and honored and glorified in the eternal life. And for Christ, every creature is subject to Him—the angels, the authorities, the powers, all the orders of men and angels are subject to Christ.

Chapter 3 Questions

1. Why should wives be submissive to their husbands?

2. Why did St. Peter instruct wives to adorn themselves inwardly rather than outwardly?

3. How are husbands to treat their wives?

4. How can we love life and see good days?

5. Why is the Lord against those who do evil?

6. In verse 15, who gives and keeps the hope to us and how can we maintain it?

4

Chapter Outline

Introduction

St. Peter begins this chapter by saying that the Lord Jesus Christ was willing to suffer for us, and because He accepted the will of the Father to suffer for us in the flesh, we ought to have the same mind—the same mentality, to submit to the will of the Father, and to accept suffering because suffering is the way to glory.

Then, he starts to speak about our lives as Christians and how the Gentiles, or the non-believers, when they see the transformation in our lives, when they see that we give up sins like drunkenness, like drinking parties, like sexual immorality—how those in the world will think it strange.

Why you are doing this? Why you are not going with them to the same dissipation? They do not understand that they will give an account to God, who will judge both the living and the dead. The "living" are those who are living according to the will of God, and the dead are those who are spiritually dead because of their involvement in the sin and pleasures of the world.

After that, St. Peter tells us that the end of time is approaching, and because of this, we need to be watchful in our prayers, we need to be fervent in our love to one another, and we need to be hospitable, because we will stand before God and give account for everything we did in our lives.

We will also give account for the gifts that we received from God and that is why we should make use of our gifts, "as good stewards of the manifold grace of God" (1 Peter 4:10). God entrusted you with a certain gift in order to serve others with this gift.

Then, St. Peter speaks about suffering for Christ, saying that when we face persecution, when we see non-Christians persecuting Christians, we should not consider it a strange thing. We should expect this because we do not have a permanent city here on earth. Instead of being troubled, it should be an opportunity for us to rejoice. Why? If we participate in the suffering of Christ, we will also participate in His glory, and not only that, but the Spirit of God will rest upon us, upon those who accept suffering to glorify God.

He concludes the chapter by speaking about the Judgment Day, that those who suffered for Christ will be rewarded and glorified, but those who do not obey the gospel will have no hope in the Second Coming of Christ.

4:1 **Therefore, since Christ suffered for us in the flesh, arm yourselves also with the same mind, for he who has suffered in the flesh has ceased from sin.** He is saying that Christ accepted to suffer in the flesh. He was born in a manger. He did not have a place to lay His head. He was persecuted during His entire life on earth, and at the end, He was crucified.

Why did He accept to suffer? He suffered for us to redeem us and to save us, because He loved us; but He also suffered because this was the will of the Father, to save us. In Gethsemane, He prayed and said, "Let it not be according to My will, but Your will" (cf. Luke 22:42).

St. Peter is saying, "If Christ suffered for us in the flesh and obeyed the will of the Father, you need to arm yourself with the same mind." I want you to notice the word, "arm," here. To "arm" is as if you are going into a war, as if suffering is our spiritual weapon by which we will win. We, as Christians should be equipped with the spiritual weapons for warfare and suffering. Therefore, we are to have this mind,

and this mentality that we are willing to suffer, so that when suffering comes, we will not be troubled by it.

Do you know why we are troubled when we hear about suffering or about persecution? It is because we did not arm ourselves with the same mind. Thus, we are refusing and rejecting the fact of suffering for righteousness' sake. But, if we armed ourselves—if we accepted this and make it acceptable to our hearts, that we should suffer for the sake of righteousness, that for us, as Christians, it is our duty to suffer for righteousness' sake—if we armed ourselves with this mind, with this mentality, which was in the Lord Jesus Christ, then, if suffering or persecution happens, we will be happy, we will be ready, and we will be equipped for that moment. Therefore, the mind that was in Christ when He suffered, this willingness to suffer, to do the will of God, should be our mind. "Arm yourselves also with the same mind."

for he who has suffered in the flesh has ceased from sin. Why should I arm myself with this? St. Peter is telling us that if we suffer in the flesh, we will cease from sin. Suffering with Christ will put an end to our connection with sin because suffering with Christ means we will enter through the narrow gate, we will not seek the pleasures of the world, and we will crucify our passions and our lusts. This is suffering with Christ.

Also, when we suffer in the flesh, we return to God; we repent. I am sure that most of us when we are sick or when we go through a difficult time, we cry to God, "Heal me, and I will repent. I know my sins and I promise I will not do it again." Thus, suffering has benefits of leading us to repentance and making us cease from sinning, "For he who has suffered in the flesh has ceased from sin."

4:2 **that he no longer should live the rest of his time in the flesh for the lusts of men, but for the will of God.** St. Peter is saying that now, since I have accepted suffering, accepted to walk in the difficult way, and accepted to enter through the narrow gate, I will not spend the rest of my life here on earth in sin, seeking the pleasures of the world, and pursuing the lusts of the flesh. No, "… he no longer should live the rest of his time in the flesh for the lusts of men, but for the will of God." Therefore, I will always say, "Thy will be done," and I will fulfill the will of God in my life.

4:3 **For we have spent enough of our past lifetime in doing the will of the Gentiles - when we walked in lewdness, lusts, drunkenness, revelries, drinking parties, and abominable idolatries.** The Gentiles are the non-believers. St. Peter is saying, "We have spent enough time sinning and living like the unbelievers. It is enough. In the past, we spent our time in the pleasures of the world and in the lusts of the flesh. Let us now repent and return back to God."

After he said that we have spent enough of our past lifetime in doing the will of the Gentiles, he mentions some sins in verse 3:

when we walked in lewdness, lusts, drunkenness, revelries, drinking parties, and abominable idolatries. Lewdness means living in impurity, living an unholy life like the unbelievers, and refers to sexual immorality. Lusts are uncleanness. It is when you lust, whether it is sexual or non-sexual lust, like gluttony, which is the lust for food. Lewdness has to do with sexual immorality. That is why we call lewdness, "impurity." Lusts have to do with all "uncleanness."

drunkenness. This refers to consuming an excess of wine or alcohol until a person gets drunk.

revelries. This refers to riots, quarreling, or fighting.

drinking parties. This refers to when people celebrate together, and part of this celebration is to consume alcohol and dance. That is why our receptions, whether wedding or graduation receptions, should not be like the nonbelievers.

St. Peter condemned drinking parties. When you have a party or a reception in which there is drinking and dancing, this is non-Christian. It is like the unbelievers. St. Peter is clearly saying, here, that we should not do this. We should not be involved in drinking parties.

abominable idolatries. This refers to the worshipping of idols, because many times when they worshiped idols, the Gentiles, the non-believers, did many of the abominations. Some of them practiced sex as part of worshipping the idols. That is why St. Peter said, "Not only idolatries, which is the worshipping of idols, is wrong, but also all the practices that are done in worshipping the idols; they are also abominations to the Lord."

St. Peter said that all these things, so that as Christians and people who have accepted to suffer for Christ, we should not be involved in such practices. As people who have accepted to enter through the narrow gate and to walk in the difficult way, we should not be involved in any of these sins.

4:4 **In regard to these, they think it strange that you do not run with them in the same flood of dissipation, speaking evil of you.** When you repent and return to God and

your friends invite you to a drinking party and you tell them, "No, I do not drink," or when they invite you to a dancing party and you tell them, "No, I do not dance," when you do not follow them, they will think it strange. They will call you names. They will say, "Why you are not doing this? Why are you not normal like the rest of the world?" They will accuse you of being abnormal and will speak evil of you.

A young man or young woman, or a teenager who refuses to date or chooses to keep their virginity, many of their friends will tell them that they are unattractive or that they do not have a normal sexual life. They put pressure on the pure and wholesome youth. Thus, St. Peter is warning us that the world outside will think it strange that you are not engaged in these sins with them any longer.

in the same flood of dissipation. This means that when these people are involved in such sins, it is like a flood of sins: drinking, dancing, sexual immorality, all these sins. Dissipation means that they do not respect God, they do not respect themselves, and they do not respect others.

That is why these people—the unbelievers or the ungodly will speak evil about the children of God, because for the unbelievers, their fun, their habits, and their enjoyment are in these activities. They cannot understand how you can live as a virgin until you get married. They will not understand how you are not drinking and dancing and dating, and how you do not use drugs. They will think it strange because, for them, that is how a person enjoys life.

But, we, the children of God, we know that the road to true happiness and true joy is when we abide in Christ and when we fulfill the will of God. The others will speak evil of you because you refused to rush into their sins.

4:5 They will give an account to Him who is ready to judge the living and the dead. Sinners, who are living an unholy and ungodly life, persecute the righteous because they refuse to engage with them in these sins. Thus, these sinners will give an account to God on Judgment Day. They will give an account to God: (1) because of their ungodly and unholy life; (2) because they persecute the righteous and pressure godly people to get involved with them in the same sins and dissipation.

When St. Peter said that God is "ready to judge the living and the dead," the living refers to those who are godly, and the dead refers to those who are spiritually dead.

4:6 For this reason the gospel was preached also to those who are dead, that they might be judged according to men in the flesh, but live according to God in the spirit. The gospel is preached to everybody, to the godly and to the ungodly, to the living and to the dead. "Dead," here, means those who are dead spiritually, like the Prodigal Son, whose father said about him, "for this my son was dead and is alive again," (Luke 15:24). If I am dead spiritually, but I hear the preaching of the gospel and I repent, I will have moved from death into life. People may speak evil about me and may judge me, but I will live according to the spirit.

For this reason the gospel was preached to those who are dead. God sent His word to those who are spiritually dead. If they accept it, what will happen to them? They might be judged according to men in the flesh, people may judge them, the ungodly may speak evil about them, but they [the penitents] will live in the spirit and according to God because they repented.

that they might be judged according to men in the flesh, but live according to God in the spirit. There is another way to understand the meaning of this. After we repent, we will be judged according to the judgment of all men in the flesh, which means that after we physically die, we will rise again in the Last Day and live according to God in the spirit.

Thus, we will face Judgment, which is death, as the Lord said to Adam, "You shall surely die" (Gen 2:17). Everybody will die. This is the judgment of men according to the flesh, but we will live according to God in the spirit.

Why is the gospel to be preached to those who are dead? Because without knowing the gospel, they cannot be judged. God sent us His word so that we would not have an excuse when we are judged, because if we did not receive the word of God, we might have an excuse. Thus, St. Peter is saying, "For this reason the gospel was preached to those who are dead." The gospel is preached to everybody, so that no one would have an excuse on Judgment Day.

those who are dead. Those who have heard the gospel and received it, while they may experience the physical death which will come upon all men, are called to live according to God in the spirit. "To live according to God in the spirit" means to fulfill the commandment of God in one's spiritual life, so that I will walk my life and live it according to the will of God in the spirit.

4:7 But the end of all things is at hand. St. Peter was speaking about the Judgment, so he said, "the end of all things is at hand." Some may argue and say, "But, St. Peter wrote this 2,000 years ago; so, how is the end of all things still at hand?" St. Peter answered this question in his second letter when he said, "that with the Lord one day is as a thousand years, and a thousand years as one day" (2 Pet 3:8). Thus, from the time of St. Peter until now, even though this was written 2,000 years ago, it is like two days. The end of all times, the end of their wrongs, the end of our sufferings, the end of our entertainment, and the end of our lives is at hand.

Maybe he is not speaking about the end of the world but the end of our personal lives—each individual person. We do not know when we will leave the world; so "the end of all things is at hand."

Therefore be serious and watchful in your prayers. I remember H.H. Pope Shenouda III of Thrice Blessed Memory told us that the main difference between the saints and us is seriousness. They took their lives seriously. They took their commitment to the Christian life seriously. That is why they became saints; but we are not taking our lives seriously. Therefore, St. Peter says, "be serious and watchful."

When you are serious and watchful, this will help and support your prayers. Be watchful in your prayers. How? When you are watchful, you see the attacks of the enemy, and every time you see the enemy's attacks are coming at you, you will cry for help; you will pray and ask God for help. When you take your life seriously and you find the many challenges in the world around you, what will you do? You will ask God for help.

Seriousness and watchfulness will help your prayers, as it is said, "Watch that you may pray, and pray that you may watch." Watch that you may pray, and pray that you may watch, but this is not enough because we need to also bear the fruit of the Spirit, which is love. That is why in verse 8 St. Peter said,

4:8 **And above all things have fervent love for one another, for 'love will cover a multitude of sins.'**

above all. St. Peter is saying that the main virtue you need to acquire in your heart is love. God is love (1 Jn 4:8; 4:16). If you want to summarize the whole Bible in one word, it would be, "love." We can summarize the Ten Commandments in two commandments: the first four commandments are to "love the Lord your God," and the last six commandments are to "love your neighbor as yourself."

There is a song that says, "the Bible in a word is love"—that is true. That is why St. Augustine said, "Love God and do whatever you want," because if you love God, you will do everything right. That is why St. Peter said, "Above all things have fervent love for one another," because when we love one another, we will be the disciples of Christ, and the

Lord told us, "By this the world will know that you are My disciples, if you love one another" (Jn 13:35).

I was reading a book recently, and this book recommended something very nice. It recommended reading 1 Corinthians, Chapter 13, and when it says, "Love does not envy, love endures everything, love accepts everything." the author suggests removing the word, "love," and putting your first name instead of it; then, read it. For example, if your name is George, you would read, "George does not envy; George puts others before himself; George endures everything." When you read it this way, you will see how we are deficient in this commandment of love. When you read it about yourself, you will make it personal, and you will see how deficient you are in your love. That is why he said, "Above all things have fervent love, zealous love, for one another."

Do you want to know if you have love for others or not? St. Peter quoted a verse from Proverbs 10:12, "Love covers all sins." Can you overlook the sins of others or are you exaggerating the sins of others? Do you speak about others' sins? Do you gossip? Do you talk with others about others' sins? If you are doing this, you do not have love in your heart.

Love covers a multitude of sins. Love covers not just one sin, but a multitude of sins, as God covered our sins by His blood and died to cover our sins. He covered our sins because He loved us. "Love covers a multitude of sins."

4:9 **Be hospitable to one another without grumbling.** At that time, many Christians were persecuted and ousted from their homes. That was why the commandment to "be hospitable" and to host one another was very much needed at that time. St. Peter said that when you do host somebody in your house and you show him hospitality, do it without grumbling or complaining, but do it with all cheerfulness.

Nowadays, when newcomers come to our churches, it is time to practice this commandment. How we are hospitable to them, how we accept them without complaining or grumbling, but with all cheerfulness, because again, that is love. If I love my brother, I will accept him in my house, and I will be hospitable to him. That is why he told us, "Be hospitable to one another without grumbling."

4:10 **As each one has received a gift, minister it to one another, as good stewards of the manifold grace of God.** He is saying that God gave each one of us different gifts. That is why he used the word "manifold."

To one person, He gave the gift of teaching; to another. He gave the gift of knowledge; to somebody else He gave the gift of healing; so, different gifts were given to different people.

You may receive one gift, or you may receive more than one gift, but nobody did not receive any gift. Everybody received at least one gift. That is why he said, "As each one," meaning that each one of us received at least one gift.

This gift was given to you not for yourself, but this gift was given to you to serve others with your gift. That is why he said, "As each one of you has received a gift, minister it to one another." Minister it and serve one another with these gifts.

St. Peter says we are to do this, "as good stewards of the manifold grace of God." These gifts are not yours, but you are just a steward. God appointed you as a steward to serve others with this gift. If you act like this gift is yours, you are unfaithful; you are acting like the owner not as a steward.

There are two virtues to being a good steward as the Lord Jesus Christ said, "Who is the wise and faithful steward" (Lk 12:42)? In order to serve one another with your gifts, you need to be wise and you need to be faithful.

Think about it this way. If you have a business and you appointed a manager to run your business, this manager is not the owner. You are the owner, but he is your steward. If he is wise, he will make a lot of profit. If he is faithful, he will give you all the profit. He will not steal the profit from you. But, if he is wise and unfaithful, he will make a lot of profit, but he will steal it from you, and if he is faithful, but not wise, yes, he is not going to steal anything, but he is not making any profit. That is why you need to be both wise and faithful in order to be a good steward.

Wise means able to make profit. Faithful means to do it for the glory of God. "As each one has received a gift, minister, *serve one another with this gift*, as good stewards of the manifold grace of God."

You should know that it is the grace of God. You did not earn this gift because the word "grace" means a free gift given to you. If we received this gift from God's grace, we did not earn it. It is a gift from God. That is why it is called gift.

We need to differentiate between the reward and the gift. You earn a reward, but a gift is given to you because of the goodness of the giver, not because of the worthiness of the receiver. The gift is given because of the goodness of the giver and not because of the worthiness of the receivers. Thus, we should not use the gift for our own [purposes], but as God's stewards.

From verse 11, St. Peter starts to give us some practical applications as to how to use the gifts for the glory of God.

4:11 **If anyone speaks, let him speak as the oracles of God. If anyone ministers, let him do it as with the ability which God supplies, that in all things God may be glorified through Jesus Christ, to whom belong the glory and the dominion forever and ever. Amen.** If you have the gift of speech or if you are an eloquent speaker, do not speak your own words, but speak the word of God. God gave you this gift in order to preach His word, in order to evangelize to others, in order to bring others to Christ and to bring others to repentance. That is why you should not use your own words, but use "the oracles of God."

If anyone ministers, let him do it as with the ability which God supplies. St. Peter means that if you are called to be a servant, whether a Sunday School servant, or a deacon, or a priest, or a bishop, or if you are serving in any capacity (if anyone ministers, if anyone is serving), let him do it as with the ability which God supplies.

We can understand this in two ways: (1) When you work hard in your service, do not say, "This is my power," or "this is my ability." No, this ability is given to you from God. God empowered you to serve Him with zeal. Thus, you should know that God supplies this ability, this power. It is not your own power. (2) If God gave you this power, you need to not be lazy. You need to be zealous in your service because God gave you this power to serve Him, to minister. Do not be lazy in your service, but be zealous, act with zeal, as God gave you this strength and this power.

that in all things God may be glorified. Do you remember when I told you about the faithful servant? The faithful servant does everything for the glory of God, not to glorify himself. Thus, when you are using your spiritual gifts, use them to glorify God, so that in all things God may be glorified, because God is the source of every spiritual gift.

through Jesus Christ. It is only through Christ that God will be glorified in our lives, in our sayings, and in our doings. I want you to notice that he said, "If anyone speaks." He was speaking about our speech. When he said, "if anyone ministers," he was speaking about our actions. Therefore, St. Peter is speaking about what we say and what we do.

It is only through Jesus Christ that God will be glorified means that when you abide in the body of Christ, the Church of Christ, when you abide in His body, you will be able to glorify God the Father.

Some people speak and some people minister, but without believing in Christ or without preaching the truth of Christ, we are not glorifying God. So, to glorify God, you need to be Christian, believing in Christ, following Christ in your actions and in your speech.

to whom belong the glory and the dominion forever and ever. Amen.
"To whom"—to Christ. It is the glory of His wisdom that teaches us to speak and the dominion of His power that enables us to act and to minister. St. Peter is talking about speaking and acting, saying that in order to speak, you need to have wisdom, and this wisdom is given to us from God, and to act, you need to have power. That is why he said, "To whom belong the glory" (the glory of wisdom) "and the dominion" (the dominion of power), which enables us to act and to glorify Him.

From verse 12, and keep in mind he was addressing people who were persecuted for Christ and for righteousness, he returns to the issue of suffering. St. Peter addressed the issue of suffering more than one time because at that time in the first century, the Christians were suffering.

4:12 Beloved, do not think it strange concerning the fiery trial which is to try you, as though some strange thing happened to you. The fiery trial refers to persecution. He is saying, "You know that you are not of this world and the world is always against you." Expect suffering as the

Lord also told us, "If you were of this world, the world would love you, but you are not of this world. That is why the world hates you" (cf. Jn 15:18–19).

Many people, when they hear about the persecution or the suffering of the Copts, question, "Why?" St. Peter is telling us, "Do not consider it strange." Although God is not the initiator of suffering, He will use suffering to try us, to test us, to purify us. God is not the one who initiates suffering but will use our suffering to try us and to purify us like gold purified by fire.

do not think it strange concerning the fiery trial. Persecution, which comes upon you and tries you, God will use to purify you, to test you; then, what should be your reaction? Many people ask, "What should we do when we hear about what is happening in Egypt right now?" Verse 13 has the answer:

4:13 but rejoice to the extent that you partake of Christ's sufferings, that when His glory is revealed, you may also be glad with exceeding joy. Do not be troubled. You need to rejoice. Why? Because, if you are persecuted for Christ, you are persecuted for the sake of righeousness, and this will make you partakers of Christ's sufferings and will qualify you for the title: "a partaker of Christ's sufferings."

What does this mean to be a partaker of Christ's sufferings? St. Peter is saying that when His glory is revealed, when He comes in His Second Coming in His glory and the glory of His Father, you will also be glad with exceeding joy. All those who suffer with Him will be glorified with Him and will be rejoicing exceedingly when Christ comes. That is why it is an opportunity for you, because you will be glorified at His Second Coming and you will also rejoice and be glad with exceeding joy.

4:14 If you are reproached for the name of Christ, blessed are you, for the Spirit of glory and of God rests upon you. On their part He is blasphemed, but on your part He is glorified. If you are reproached, if you are persecuted, if they revile you because you are Christian, or for the name of Christ, you ought to be happy! Happy are you, blessed are you! The sufferer for Christ is happy because the glory of Christ awaits him, and God's Spirit is with him. If you are reproached for the name of Christ, blessed are you. Why are you blessed? "For the Spirit of glory and of God rests upon you."

the Spirit of glory and of God rests upon you. God will support you with His Spirit for you to be able to endure this suffering, and the Spirit of glory to be glorified will rest upon you. This Spirit is the Spirit of Christ Himself. That is why he said, "The Spirit of glory and the Spirit of God."

You will be glorified as the Spirit of God is comforting you, as St. Paul said in 2 Corinthians, Chapter 1: "Blessed be the Lord Jesus Christ who has comforted us in all our tribulations." This Spirit, the Comforter, the Holy Spirit, will comfort you and will also glorify you.

On their part He is blasphemed, but on your part He is glorified. Those who persecute you will blaspheme the name of Christ. I am sure you hear what they are saying about Christ, and how they blaspheme His name. However, when you endure suffering for His name, you are glorifying God. What a big difference there is between the persecutors who blaspheme the name of Christ, and we who are persecuted, who glorify the name of Christ by accepting this suffering? On their part He is blasphemed, but on your part, He [the name of Christ] is glorified.

4:15 **But let none of you suffer as a murderer, a thief, an evildoer, or as a busybody in other people's matters.** He is saying that you will be glorified if you suffer for righteousness's sake, and you will be glorified if you suffer for the name of Christ; but if you are suffering as an evildoer, you deserve this suffering and are receiving the punishment of your evildoing. St. Peter is providing an example that if you are a murderer and are now in prison, you should not complain, because you are

reaping the fruit of my deeds.

Then, St. Peter says to us, "You, as a Christian should not suffer as a murderer, as a thief, as an evildoer, or as a busybody." What does it mean to be a "busybody?" When you interfere in other people's business, or you are a busybody in other peoples' matters. Many people like to interfere in other peoples' lives and in other peoples' matters, but St. Peter is saying that this is a sin, equal to an evildoer, to a murderer, to a thief.

St. Peter has a nice story about not meddling in other people's business; so that is why he mentioned this. Do you remember when after the resurrection of Christ, the Lord asked Peter, "Do you love Me more than these?" St. Peter replied, "Yes Lord; You know that I love You" (John 21:15). The Lord told him, "Follow Me." After the Lord told St. Peter to follow Him, who else followed the Lord? St. John did. Peter looked at the Lord and said, "Why is he following us" (cf. Jn 21:20)? He interfered in John's life, so the Lord told him, "What is it your business? If I want him to remain until I come in My Second Coming, what is this to you? You follow Me" (cf. Jn 21:21–22). The Lord taught St. Peter a lesson, to not interfere in other peoples' lives. That is why St. Peter (because he remembers this lesson very well) said, "Let none of you suffer as an evildoer, as a murderer, as a thief, or as a busybody in other people's matters."

4:16 Yet if anyone suffers as a Christian, let him not be ashamed, but let him glorify God in this matter. If I were a murderer and they put me in prison, I would be ashamed, and maybe I would try to hide it from everybody, but St. Peter is telling us: "If you suffer for the name of Christ, if they put chains on your hands and put you in prison because you are a Christian, do not be ashamed. Rather, you need to glory in this, that you are now suffering for Christ."

let him glorify God in this matter. Let him glorify God who gives him the honor to suffer. God will also give us a great reward for suffering for His name's sake.

In the Book of Acts, Chapter 5, when the apostles were physically attacked, we read that they returned rejoicing because they were considered worthy to suffer shame for His name's sake. The apostles were essentially saying, "We are not worthy to suffer shame for the name of Christ; it is an honor for us." This is exactly what St. Peter is telling us: "Do not be ashamed if you suffer for Christ but glorify God because He gave you this honor to suffer for His name, and He will also give you glory in His Second Coming."

4:17 For the time has come for judgment to begin at the house of God; and if it begins with us first, what will be the end of those who do not obey the gospel of God? St. Peter is saying that the end of the time is at hand. What does that mean? It means the Judgment. Since the judgment will come very soon, the time has come for Judgment, and God will judge His children first.

In Matthew 25, He puts the sheep on His right side and the goats on His left side—the godly people on His right side and the wicked on His left side. With whom does He begin? He starts with those on His right side. Thus, Judgment will begin at the house of God means that the righteous will be judged first.

and if it begins with us first, what will be the end of those who do not obey the gospel of God? If God will judge His children first, those who do not believe in Him, those who rejected Him, those who refused Him, what kind of judgment will they suffer and endure? Thus, in verse 18, St. Peter quotes Proverbs 11:31.

4:18 Now 'If the righteous one is scarcely saved, where will the ungodly and the sinner appear?' If the righteous is called to judgment, what shall be the fate of the disobedient and the non-believer? If the righteous person must suffer and will be judged, and God will chasten and discipline him, if all these things happen to the righteous, what hope is there for the wicked? If the righteous one is scarcely saved—he suffers, he is disciplined, and he is chastened by God, where will the ungodly and the sinner appear?

Do you remember the story of the rich man and Lazarus? Abraham said to the rich man, "Remember that Lazarus, in his life on earth, suffered a lot. Now, he is comforted. You lived a life of fun, entertainment, and pleasures. That is why you are tortured, now" (cf. Luke 16:25). Thus, if the righteous one is scarcely saved, where will the ungodly and the sinner appear?

4:19 Therefore let those who suffer according to the will of God commit their souls to Him in doing good, as to a faithful Creator. Let those who suffer—not for doing evil, but for righteousness' sake, let them keep on in doing well. Do not give up. Do not say, "I am doing well, but I will suffer; so, why should I continue to do well?" St. Peter is saying, "No. If you are suffering for the name of Christ according to the will of God, commit yourself to Him in doing well; commit yourself to God in doing well." Thus, by doing well, you are committing yourself to God. By keeping the commandment of God, you are committing yourself to God.

Commit yourself to God who will take care of your soul. He sees your suffering. He hears your crying.

Therefore, commit yourselves to the care of God who is our faithful Creator, who sees our suffering and is faithful to us, His children. That is why we trust His truth, His love, His power. We trust Him, and in our sufferings, we are not troubled because we trust our faithful Creator.

~~~~~~~~

Chapter 4 Questions

1. According to Saint Peter, why is it necessary for us to suffer in the flesh?

2. Why was the gospel preached also to those who are dead?

3. What is the apostle urging us to do since the end of all things is at hand?

4. What is the significance of the virtue of love compared to all the other virtues?

5. Under which condition should the believers be hospitable to one another?

6. What is the condition for speaking?

7. What is the condition for ministering? Why?

8. What should we do when we experience the fiery trial?

9. Why are the believers blessed when they are reproached for the name of Christ?

10. What should we do if we suffer as Christians?

~~~~~~~~

5

Chapter Outline

- Shepherd the flock (1-4)
- Submit to God, resist the devil (5-11)
- Farewell and peace (12-14)

Introduction

This final chapter starts with some commandments to the clergy and bishops and to their flock. St. Peter gave general instructions to the people to humble themselves under the mighty hand of God so that God may exalt them and elevate them, because God resists the proud, but He gives grace to the humble.

St. Peter also advised them to be watchful and to be sober, because the devil is like a roaring lion. He told them, "You need to resist the devil and he will flee from you." This is the way we need to follow in spiritual warfare to resist the devil and the devil will flee.

He concluded this letter with a prayer that God may establish and strengthen them and commanded them to greet one another with a holy kiss, or a kiss of love, which is what we do during the Divine Liturgy.

5:1 The elders who are among you I exhort, I who am a fellow elder and a witness of the sufferings of Christ, and also a partaker of the glory that will be revealed. The word, "elder," here, does not mean aged people but rather refers to the clergy [the priesthood], as it is also made clear in verse 2 when St. Peter instructs them to shepherd the flock of God. St. Peter himself was considered a clergyman— a priest, because when the Lord Jesus Christ gave the Holy Spirit to the disciples the authority to bind and to loose sins on earth, that was when God ordained them into the priesthood (cf. Mt 16:19).

The elders who are among you I exhort. This exhortation is for the clergy. St. Peter is saying, "I who am a fellow elder and also a clergyman, I exhort you as one of you." We read this exhortation at the ordination of new priests. The bishop reads the same exhortation to the new presbyter on the day of his ordination.

witness of the sufferings of Christ. St. Peter was an eyewitness of Christ's sufferings and also of His resurrection. In the first century, eyewitnesses were very, very important to affirm the truth about the sufferings and resurrection of our Lord Jesus Christ. Therefore, this is the witness of a person who was with the Lord Jesus Christ and who was an eyewitness of His sufferings and His resurrection.

partaker of the glory that will be revealed. He is telling them, "We the clergy. If we do our mission in faithfulness and with wisdom, we will be partakers of the glory that will be revealed in the Second Coming of Christ."

Yes, all the believers will be glorified, but, in heaven, there will be different levels of glorification. We read in 1 Corinthians, Chapter 15: "One star differs from another star in glory." In the Book of Revelation (cf. Chapters 4–6) we find there is glory for the twenty-four priests, there is another glory for the four creatures, and another glory for the angels; so, everybody has their own glory.

One of the observations about the twenty-four priests mentioned in the Book of Revelation is that while everybody is standing around the throne of God (even in the Divine Liturgy we say, "Before whom stand all the angels, the archangels, the principalities, and the authorities"), the only group that was sitting around the throne of God were the twenty-four Priests. That is why some of the Fathers have said that the glory of the twenty-four priests is different than the glory of the rest of heaven, and that is why St. Peter is telling them, "I am also a partaker of the glory that will be revealed when Christ comes."

5:2 Shepherd the flock of God which is among you, serving as overseers, not by compulsion but willingly, not for dishonest gain but eagerly. This is the commandment— the exhortation that St. Peter is giving them: "Shepherd, the flock of God." He uses the word "shepherd" because this is the same word that the Lord used with St. Peter when He told him, "Peter son of Jonah, do you love Me more than these?" Peter answered Him, "Yes Lord, You know that I love You." So, He told him, "Tend to My flock," (John 21:15-16) or shepherd My flock.

As Peter received this exhortation from the Lord's mouth, so he is also exhorting the clergy to shepherd. In order to understand what the word, "shepherd," means, we, need to study Psalm 23: "The Lord is my Shepherd." We should follow the example of the Good Shepherd—our Lord Jesus Christ, how He made David not want nor need anything. As God's stewards, we, too, should follow the footsteps of the Good Shepherd, the Lord Jesus Christ.

Also, in order to understand what the word, "shepherd," means, we need to study John, Chapter 10, the chapter on the Good Shepherd. During the ordination of a patriarch, the Holy Gospel that is read on that day is John 10, "The Good Shepherd." One of the most important verses in this chapter is that the good shepherd always lays down his life for his flock.

Thus, St. Peter is telling the clergy, "You need to shepherd God's flock because this flock pertains to God and He trusted you to tend His people, to tend His flock. Therefore, you need to shepherd them. You need to be ready to die for your people." That is what the word, "shepherd," means, and a good shepherd lays down his life for his people.

Shepherd the flock of God. This flock is not ours, but God's, and we are stewards of God; we are God's servants. He entrusted us to shepherd His own children.

which is among you. He is saying, "You need to shepherd the flock in the churches, wherever you are."

serving as overseers. The word, "overseer" means bishop. "Over," in Greek is "epi" and "seer" is "scope," like the word telescope or microscope. So, "scope" means "seer" and "epi" means "over;" so, "overseer" is "episcopos." The word "episcopos" in Greek means "bishop." Therefore, serving as overseers is serving as bishops. In this context, we can say that St. Peter was addressing the bishops.

Why is the bishop called an overseer? Because he watches over the flock of God, as if he is watching over all their needs, attending to all their needs, and providing for the needs of the people of God.

not by compulsion but willingly. St. Peter is saying, "When you accepted to be a servant of God, to be a clergyman, to be a bishop, since you accepted this responsibility and this duty, you need to do it cheerfully, not by compulsion, not out of obligation, but out of love." When we serve, we do not serve because we must serve or because we are obligated to serve, but we need to serve because of the love of God that is in our hearts; we should do it cheerfully, and willingly. Thus, the second commandment is to serve, "not by compulsion but willingly."

not for dishonest gain but eagerly. Again, my motivation should not be for love of gain, love of money, or love of collecting money. This should not be the motivation of the clergy. Rather, we should serve with enthusiasm, with eagerness, with dedication, and commitment. So, St. Peter said three things regarding service: (1) not by compulsion but willingly; (2) not for dishonest gain but eagerly; (3) nor as being lords over those entrusted to you, but being examples to the flock as discussed in verse 3.

5:3 **nor as being lords over those entrusted to you, but being examples to the flock.** St. Peter is saying: "God appointed you as an overseer, but do not feel that you are the master and the people are your servants. That is absolutely unacceptable to God.

You should know that these people are the people of God and they were entrusted to you. Thus, do not act as lords over them. Do not behave in a dictatorship style. If God has appointed you as an overseer, the purpose of this appointment is for you to be an example that others may follow." The leadership of the clergy is not to lord over the people, but to be an example that the people may follow.

St. John Chrysostom used to pray and ask for his congregation by saying to the Lord: "Your servants, my masters." St. John Chrysostom considered the people to be his masters, but the people are the servants of God." He says, "Your servants, my masters," because the true leader, the true clergy, the true bishop, is the one who serves, not the one who is asking to be served, as the Lord Jesus Christ said, "The Son of Man did not come to be served but to serve" (Mt 20:28; Mk 10:45). He also washed the feet of His disciples and told them, "As I washed your feet, go and wash the feet of one another" (cf. John 13:14).

Thus, St. Peter is telling them three important commandments here:

You need to shepherd: (1) Not by compulsion but willingly; (2) Not for dishonest gain but eagerly; (3) Nor acting as lords over the flock of God, but being examples to the flock.

We need to watch ourselves very, very carefully, because the responsibility of being an example to be followed is a huge responsibility. If we walk in the wrong way, all the congregation will follow in the wrong way, and this is a huge responsibility for the clergy.

5:4 And when the Chief Shepherd appears, you will receive the crown of glory that does not fade away. This refers to the Lord Jesus Christ in His Second Coming. Who is the Chief Shepherd? The Lord Jesus Christ Himself is the Good Shepherd—the Shepherd of the shepherds.

This verse implies what? It implies accountability. You will give an account to the Chief Shepherd in His Second Coming, and if He finds you faithful and wise, if He finds that you shepherded the flock of God willingly, cheerfully, with eagerness, being an example to them, you will receive the crown of glory—the eternal reward that does not fade away.

The glory of the world is temporary, transient, and fades away, but the eternal glory is permanent. Thus, he is telling them, "If you are faithful and wise, you will receive the eternal crown, but if not, you will not receive it."

By the end of verse 4, St. Peter has finished the exhortations to the clergy. From verse 5, he starts giving exhortations to the younger people.

5:5 Likewise you younger people, submit yourselves to your elders. Yes, all of you be submissive to one another, and be clothed with humility, for God resists the proud, but gives grace to the humble.

younger. This can be understood in many ways. It can be understood to mean younger in position; for example, like how the deacon submits to the priest, the priest submits to the bishop, the bishop submits to the patriarch, and so on. Thus, "younger" can mean either younger in position or younger in age or younger in ordination. Within the same rank, maybe the one younger in ordination should submit to the one older in ordination. We follow this rule in monasteries where the novices submit to the elder monks.

submit yourselves to your elders. If this instruction is for the deacons, for the servants, and for the priests to submit to the higher ranks, it is definitely for everybody, and definitely for the whole congregation to submit to their clergy.

St. Paul, in his Epistle to the Hebrews 13:17, says to "submit to those who are in charge of you" and then, gives a very, very good reason why we need to submit: "That they may do their service without groaning, because this will not be beneficial for you."

When you are in submission and you obey your priest or your clergy, he will perform his service cheerfully, with happiness, but if you give your priest or your clergy a hard time all the time, he will do his service with groaning. When the clergy are groaning in their service, this will not be beneficial for you because the productivity of any person increases when he is happy.

Nehemiah 8:10 says: "The joy of the Lord is your strength." When we are happy and joyful, our productivity and service will be more and more. However, if people give the clergy a hard time, the clergy will groan, and their productivity and their service will definitely decrease. This will not be beneficial for you. That is why St. Peter said, "Likewise you younger people, submit yourselves to your elders."

yes, all of you be submissive to one another, and be clothed with humility. Be submissive to one another is a commandment to those who should be submissive. What do I mean by this? Children should be submissive to their parents. But, when he says to be submissive to one another, he did not mean for parents to be submissive to children, but he intended that children be submissive to parents.

Younger people should be submissive to older people. However, here, he did not mean that the older should also be submissive to the younger. Students should be submissive to teachers, but by saying, "be submissive to one another," here, he does not mean that teachers should be submissive to their students, because if we reverse the hierarchy, things will not go right. If we reverse the hierarchy, things will not go right.

St. Peter said, "be submissive to one another," but the commandment of submission is very, very hard to follow for many people. Why? It needs humbleness. One major obstacle before submission is ego or pride. It is very difficult for proud people to submit. That is why St. Peter said, "be submissive to one another and be clothed with humility."

be clothed with humility. To be clothed means like wrapping yourself in humility, as if humility becomes part of who you are; you are wrapped in humility, and you are enclosed by humility. Without humbleness, you cannot be submissive.

St. Peter gives a very good reason why we should be submissive and why we should clothe ourselves with this humility. He says:

for God resists the proud, but gives grace to the humble. This is from Proverbs 3:34. God resists the proud, but gives grace to the humble.

St. Peter is saying, "What is the sin that made Satan fall? It is the sin of pride. Why were Adam and Eve cast out of the Garden of Eden? Because of the sin of pride, God resists the proud." Why does God resist the proud? When we commit any other sin, we flee from God; we escape from God, but the sin of pride opposes itself to God. In any other sin, we escape from God, but the prideful person actually opposes God. Therefore, God, also in return, opposes the proud. He resists the proud. As for the humble, He gives them grace. So, if you want to receive the grace of God, humble yourself and be submissive. To be submissive means to be ready always to give up your own will.

Think about why children fight with their parents, why couples fight with each other, why students disagree with their teachers, why in churches we sometimes have conflicts among church members or between congregation and clergy. What is the reason behind all of this? It is either my will or your will— the fight and who will win at the end.

It is like a power struggle, and a power struggle is a sign of what? It is a sign of pride, not a sign of humbleness. That is why he said to clothe yourselves with humility and be ready to give up your will. God resists the proud, but He will give grace to the humble.

I can say that humbleness is the vessel for all graces. When you are humble before God, He will give you the fruit of the Holy Spirit, the gifts of the Holy Spirit, and all other graces.

5:6 Therefore humble yourselves under the mighty hand of God, that He may exalt you in due time. Many times, we are afraid that if we humble ourselves and become submissive, people may take advantage of us. But St. Peter is saying that when you humble yourself, you are not humbling yourself to the other person, but you are humbling yourself under the mighty hand of God. He uses the word "mighty" because he is saying, "Your God is a mighty God. He will defend you. He will protect you. He will not allow anybody to take advantage of you. If He allows somebody to take advantage of you, it will be a school for you to grow in a certain virtue that it will end up for your benefit; so, humble yourself."

When you humble yourself, you are under the mighty hand of God. What will you receive in return? God will exalt you in due time. "In due time," means in His own time, not in your time. Many times, we say, "I humbled myself, I submitted, but I have not seen any fruit, yet. I have not seen any exaltation, yet." That is why St. Peter is telling you, "God will exalt you. He definitely will, but when? In due time, when God sees it is proper for you to be exalted."

God is a mighty God. He exalts and He also casts down. He lifts the humble as St. Mary said in her Magnificat (known as the Ode of the Theotokos or the Song of Mary, in which she magnified the Lord, mentioned in the Holy Gospel in Luke 1:46–55.), "He has put down the mighty from their thrones, and exalted the lowly" (Lk 1:52). God lifts the humble. God will exalt you in His own time, not in your time.

5:7 Casting all your care upon Him, for He cares for you. I previously told you, one of the obstacles of submission is the anxiety or the fear that others may take advantage of us. The word, "care," here, means worry or anxiety. St. Peter is telling them, "If you are anxious about something, if you are worried about people taking advantage of you, if you are worried that you will lose your rights when you humble yourself, do not worry. Just cast all your worries, cast all your anxieties upon Him.

for He cares for you. God is a Good Shepherd. He cares for you. David experienced God as a Good Shepherd, and said, "The Lord is my shepherd; I shall not want" (Psalm 23:1). King Saul could not take advantage of David although he was hunting him to kill him, but David cast his care, his worries, and his anxiety upon God and God took care of him. David was submissive to King Saul and humbled himself before King Saul, but God took care of David.

Thus, St. Peter is telling us, "Be

submissive, be humble, have no fear nor any worries because God cares for you. All you need to do is to cast your care upon Him, and God cares for you."

5:8 **Be sober, be vigilant; because your adversary the devil walks about like a roaring lion, seeking whom he may devour.** St. Peter is saying, "Be watchful. Satan is a deceiver and if you are not watchful, he can steal your humbleness from your heart and can attack you with pride." That is how he deceived our mother Eve. He tricked her and told her that God does not want her best interest. "Eat from this tree and you will be similar to God; you will be like Him" (cf. Genesis 3:5). Thus, she was deceived and ate from the fruit, and that is why she was driven out of the garden.

While you are practicing humbleness and submission, St. Peter is telling you to be watchful, be vigilant, and be sober, because our adversary, the devil, is the deceiver, and he walks about like a roaring lion, like a roaring lion searching for his prey. There is a connection here between being watchful and casting our care upon the Lord Jesus Christ, because when we are worried, when we are afraid or anxious, usually, we become more watchful. For example, if I am worried that a robber may come and steal from my house, I will be watchful. If I am

worried or anxious about my exams, I will be more watchful. Thus, St. Peter is telling us, "If you have worries, be watchful. Be vigilant in prayer. That is what you need to do. The more you are worried, the more you need to cast your care upon God in prayer. Be sober, be vigilant, and be prayerful."

Your adversary walks about like a roaring lion. It is as if he is saying, "Be vigilant, sleep no more, spend the whole night in prayer." Of course, not literally, but he means do not sleep spiritually. Rather, be vigilant all the time and walk in the day (spiritually) all the time. Do not walk in the darkness of night.

roaring lion. This means full of anger, full of rage. Satan is very, very angry and is searching for any prey to devour. "Like a roaring lion, seeking whom he may devour," because the lion, while hunting, only roars when it springs. The devil is cautious and does not give warning of his approach. That is why we need to be watchful. We need to be watchful because the devil is very, very cautious in attacking us and he is also a deceiver.

This also indicates that the devil is bound, because if the devil was not bound, he would find many, many people to devour. The fact that he is walking about like a roaring lion seeking and searching, this means his abilities are limited, which assures us that Satan is bound, because God bound him through the cross.

5:9 **Resist him, steadfast in the faith, knowing that the same sufferings are experienced by your brotherhood in the world.** The most successful way to win in your spiritual warfare is to resist. The words "resist him" were also used by St. James in his epistle when he said, "Resist Satan and he will flee from you" (James 4:7). St. Peter is saying, "Resist him, steadfast in the faith"; so, if you want to win in any spiritual warfare, the key for victory is to resist.

The Desert Fathers said that Satan is like a dog. When a dog approaches the butcher shop, if the butcher kicked it out several times, he would not return. In the same way, if we strike Satan with the rock of the cross (that is how to resist him), Satan will not come again. He will flee away and leave you alone. Therefore, keep resisting Satan and he will leave.

"Resist him steadfast in faith," meaning that you resist him [the devil] while you are confident in God. Make your confidence in God steadfast, that God is on your side. God is a mighty God. He will give you victory. At the end, He will give you victory.

In any war, when the war begins, especially if it is between equals, nobody knows who will win at the end. However, if the war is not between equals, once the war starts, or even before the war starts, we know who will win because the stronger will defeat the weaker. In the same way, in our spiritual warfare, we are stronger in God than the devil. That is why before we start our spiritual warfare, we know the outcome, and we know we are victorious in the Lord Jesus Christ.

Satan may try to make you believe that you will be defeated, that you will not win, but St. Peter is telling you to be steadfast in faith. Know that the outcome is victory if you are steadfast in the Lord Jesus Christ. Although Satan is deviously seeking to swallow you up, both your soul and your body, if you resist him steadfastly in faith, you will win at the end.

"Knowing that the same sufferings are experienced by your brotherhood in the world." At that time, all the churches in the world faced persecution and sufferings. St. Peter is telling them, "Your sufferings are not unusual, but your brethren, Christians everywhere in the world, are also suffering." Why the suffering? Because Satan is walking about like a roaring lion and is triggering persecution against the churches.

While we are being persecuted, we should know that if we resist Satan and remain steadfast in our faith, we will win at the end. So, do not be defeated, do not be desperate, do not lose faith, do not lose hope under suffering, but be steadfast and know that all Christians, all those who want to live godly in the Lord Jesus Christ, will be persecuted. These sufferings are not unusual, but your brethren, the Christians everywhere, suffer as you do.

5:10 But may the God of all grace, who called us to His eternal glory by Christ Jesus, after you have suffered a while, perfect, establish, strengthen and settle you. Now, when he mentioned sufferings, St. Peter felt the need to pray for them. Thus, he is now appealing to the God of all grace—to God who bestows upon us all graces. In the time of suffering, we need the grace of God to be able to endure, to be able to have peace, to be able to have joy even amid suffering. That is why he is appealing to the God of all grace.

St. Peter is telling us: "It is God who called you to eternal glory. Do you think God will call you to eternal glory, and then will not accomplish His calling? If God called you to eternal glory, He will definitely not let His purpose fall short of completion; then, you will be glorified. You will be the winner. You will be the victor."

Do not ever think that those who persecute us will win; they will never win. God called us to eternal glory and God will fulfill His calling. He will never let His call or His purpose fall short of completion.

God of all grace, who called us to His eternal glory by Christ Jesus. God called us through Jesus Christ because He is the only way to the Father. That is why if you do not believe in Jesus Christ, you are not called to eternal glory, and you cannot inherit eternal glory. Only those who believe in the Son of God, only those who believe that Jesus Christ is God, only those who believe in His sufferings, and in His death, and in His resurrection, it is only those who will receive the eternal glory. God called us to eternal glory by Christ Jesus.

after you have suffered a while. St. Peter is saying that your suffering is temporary. God called you—and called you to what? What is the end of this calling or what is the purpose? It is the glory. But what is the way? The way is suffering, but this suffering is temporary, while our glory is eternal.

We can say that the call, the purpose of the call, and the way (which is suffering), are connected to each other. God called us. To what did He call us? He called us to eternal glory. And what is the way? The way is through suffering. If we suffer with Him, we will be glorified with Him. All of this is founded on what? It is founded on the grace of God. That is why St. Peter said, "the God of all grace." Our suffering is for a season and it will be soon over, but our glory is eternal.

perfect. To "perfect" means that God may supply your every need. God will provide you with anything you want in your spiritual warfare to resist the devil. He will leave nothing wanting. He will leave nothing wanted.

establish. To establish is to build up. We say, "We established a church in this city," meaning that we built a church. So that God may "establish" you; so that He may build you up and confirm you and make you grow.

strengthen. He will strengthen you in might because we need to be mighty in our spiritual warfare. Thus, He will strengthen you in your inner man by His Spirit, so that you will not be afraid of the devil, our enemy, or the roaring lion.

and settle you. To settle means to make you firm, to make you steadfast, to make you unshakable, to make you stable—stability. These are the four prayers: perfect, strengthen, settle, and establish you.

Though you are called to be watchful and though you are called to resist the devil, but without the grace of God, you cannot do either. That is why it is God who must do all things in you.

God will perfect you, will strengthen you, will settle you, and will establish you. You cannot watch and you cannot resist the devil without God perfecting, establishing, strengthening, and settling you.

5:11 To Him be the glory. The same God who will strengthen us, to Him and to Him alone be glory, not to ourselves. When you win, when you overcome Satan, do not glorify yourself. Do not say, "I am strong and that is why I won in my spiritual warfare." No. You should render the glory to God because it is God who made you overcome and defeat Satan. To Him is the glory. God who started and who called us, He Himself will also complete within us the work of our spiritual warfare.

and the dominion forever and ever. Amen. Dominion means to be our Lord, to be our God. He is a mighty God, and because He has the dominion, that is why He can perfect us. Because He has the dominion, He can perfect us and strengthen us. The last three verses of this chapter are the conclusion, and as usual, final chapters include a farewell and benediction.

5:12 By Silvanus, our faithful brother as I consider him, I have written to you briefly, exhorting

and testifying that this is the true grace of God in which you stand. Silvanus is another name for Silas. He was a friend and companion of St. Paul and had accompanied him on many missionary trips. Silas penned this letter. He transcribed it for St. Peter, who described him as a "faithful brother," which may imply that St. Peter had little personal acquaintance with Silvanus. However, because Silvanus had been with St. Paul on his missionary trips, St. Peter trusted him and considered him as a faithful brother. It may also be that at that time St. Paul was imprisoned, so, he sent Silvanus with a recommendation to St. Peter, and St. Peter kept Silvanus with him and considered him as a faithful brother based on the recommendation of St. Paul. Thus, St. Peter sent this letter by Silvanus.

I have written to you briefly. St. Peter's epistles are considerably shorter than St. Paul's epistles.

exhorting. What was the purpose of writing this letter? The reason is "to exhort you, to give you some advice and instructions as to how you are to behave in this world, and to testify that this is the true grace of God in which you stand, and to testify to you as eyewitness that the gospel that you received, the gospel in which you believed, the gospel that you accepted, the gospel that was preached to you, is the true gospel. This is the true message. As an eyewitness, I am telling you that the gospel which has been preached to you and you have accepted, is the true message of God."

St. Peter is testifying to them that this is the true grace of God in which they stand, and he described the gospel or the word of preaching as "grace," because it gives us the grace of knowing God.

5:13 She who is in Babylon, elect together with you, greets you; and so does Mark my son. What is Babylon? There are many interpretations and disagreements among the scholars and Bible commentators about what St. Peter meant by "Babylon." Some scholars said that he may have been referring to his wife, because, usually, salutations are from individuals. However, by saying, "elect together with you," this indicates that it is not only his wife that is elected, but there are many, many others. That is why other scholars disagreed with the opinion that Babylon, here, refers to his wife.

Other people have said that Babylon, here, refers to the Chaldean capital, Iraq, but other people say that St. Peter did not go there, or at that time, he was not there. Still others say that maybe Babylon, here, refers to Rome, before his martyrdom. Others question why St. Peter would use "Babylon" in reference to Rome. He should simply use the word "Rome." Also, other people say that St. Peter was not in Rome at that time.

The most acceptable interpretation in the Coptic Orthodox Church is that Babylon, here, refers to Egypt, because one of Egypt's old names is Babylon, and also because St. Peter said, "and so does Mark my son."

Mark my son. Mark, here, is in reference to St. Mark, the founder of the Church in Egypt. Thus, because St. Peter mentioned Babylon in addition to St. Mark, he meant that "she [the Church of Alexandria—the Coptic Orthodox Church] who is in Babylon [in Egypt], elect together with you (because God chose the Christians, the Copts of Egypt: "Blessed is Egypt My people" (Isaiah 19:25); so, we are elect and called to eternal glory with you) greets you, sends her [the Coptic Orthodox Church] greetings, and so does Mark my son.

Why did he call Mark his son? Because St. Peter's wife was the cousin of St. Mark's father, St. Peter was like his uncle. In terms of both age and relation, he described Mark as his son. This is the Mark who is St. Mark that preached Christianity in Egypt and is the author of the second account of the Holy Gospel.

5:14 **Greet one another with a kiss of love.** This is the apostolic benediction, which we use in the Divine Liturgy in the Prayer of Reconciliation when we say, "Greet one another with a holy kiss." St. Peter is saying, "Greet one another with a kiss of love," which is a sign of unity and oneness.

Peace to you all who are in Christ Jesus. Amen. "Who are in Christ Jesus" is a reference to the true Christians. "Peace to you all among all the sufferings and among all the persecutions." The most needed gift is the gift of peace, and that is why he concluded the letter by telling them, "Peace to you all who are in Christ Jesus. Amen."

Chapter 5 Questions

1. What are the terms that the Orthodox Church is using for: Elders and Overseers?

2. What should the Elders do & what they should avoid in their ministry? What kind of reward will be for them?

3. What kind of attitude is the Church expecting from the youth? Why?

4. What are the armors that the believers can use in fighting the devil?

5. "Satan is bound"; how do you prove this from the chapter?

6. What is Babylon?

The Second Epistle of Peter

AUTHOR: St. Peter. It is clear from 2 Peter 1:1 in the salutation that St. Peter is the author of this letter. St. Peter was one of the twelve disciples. Also in 1:14, St. Peter referred to a special revelation or prophesy about his martyrdom, when the Lord told him, "When you were young you girded yourself, but when you are old, somebody will gird you and carry you to where you do not want to be" (cf. John 21:18-19). Another event that St. Peter mentions in this letter is the Transfiguration: "We were with Him on the Holy Mountain, and we heard a voice coming from Heaven saying, 'This is My beloved Son in whom I am well pleased'" (1:18-19). When we read Matthew 17:1-9, we see that Peter was one of the three disciples that went with the Lord up the high Mount [of Transfiguration]. Also, St. Peter refers to the first epistle that he wrote to them, as we read in 2 Peter 3:1, in which he also acknowledged acquaintances with St. Paul, as he mentions in 2 Peter 3:15. It is for all these reasons that we believe that the author of the Second Epistle is St. Peter himself.

PLACE & TIME: In 2 Peter 1:14, St. Peter mentions that his death would be very soon, and since we know that he was martyred at the hands of Nero, and Nero committed suicide in AD 68, then this Epistle must be dated before that time—before AD 68, and before the martyrdom of St. Peter, of course, and that is why we can say that this letter was probably written around AD 67. It may also be that this letter was written while he was in prison in Rome. Therefore, we can say that the place of this letter's writing was Rome and the time was around AD 67 before St. Peter's martyrdom.

RECIPIENT OF THIS LETTER

Pilgrims of the Dispersion

In 2 Peter 3:1, he tells them, "This is the second letter I write to you." Addressing them this way implies that he is addressing the Second Epistle to the same people to whom he addressed the First Epistle.

When we read 1 Peter 1, we see that he addressed that letter to the Christian pilgrims who were living in Pontus, Galicia, Cappadocia, Asia, and Bithynia, and these five provinces were in Asia Minor, which is now Turkey. Therefore, St. Peter addressed both letters to the Christian pilgrims in these five provinces in Turkey, which was at that time known as Asia Minor.

PURPOSE FOR WRITING THIS LETTER

As we will study together, St. Peter realized that his death (his departure or his martyrdom) was at hand—very soon, so he wanted to give them a reminder to stir them up in godly living. He told them that he wanted this reminder to remain with them even after his death. This shows us what a faithful father and sincere apostle he was. He felt a responsibility toward them even after his death. That is why he wanted to leave them with a reminder to encourage them and to motivate them to live godly lives, even after his death.

THEME

He wanted to remind them to live a godly life. In 2 Peter 3:17-18, he uses these two words: "beware" and "grow." This was a warning, and at the same time, an encouragement to grow. He is warning against false teachers and false prophets, and also motivating the people to grow in their relationship with God.

OUTLINE

This is a very short epistle of only three chapters. Chapter 1 starts with an introduction and followed by a discourse about growing in the grace and knowledge of God. One of the most important passages in Chapter 1 is how St. Peter encourages us to add to our faith. He tells us we need to add to our faith: to faith add virtue, to virtue add knowledge, to knowledge add self-control, to self-control add perseverance, to perseverance add godliness, to godliness add brotherly kindness, to brotherly kindness [add] love. Thus, you need to add; that is growing. Therefore, the theme of the first chapter is growth, grace, and knowledge.

In the second chapter, St. Peter warns the people of false teachers and false prophets. In the third chapter, he encourages them to look forward to the Second Coming of the Lord—the return of the Lord. I want you to know this theological term: the "Parousia," which means the Second Coming of Christ—the Parousia of the Lord.

OUTLINE OF 2 PETER

Chapter 1
- Greeting the faithful (1-4)
- Fruitful growth in the faith (5-11)
- St. Peter's approaching death (12-15)
- The trustworthy prophetic word (16-21)

Chapter 2
- Destructive doctrines (1-3)
- Doom of false teachers (4-11)
- Depravity of false teachers (12-17)
- Deceptions of false teachers (18-22)

Chapter 3
- God's promise is not slack (1-9)
- The day of the Lord (10-13)
- Be steadfast (14-18)

1

Chapter Outline

- Greeting the faithful (1-4)
- Fruitful growth in the faith (5-11)
- St. Peter's approaching death (12-15)
- The trustworthy prophetic word (16-21)

Introduction

St. Peter encourages the people to grow in the precious gifts they received from God (verses 3 and 4). From verses 5 to 11, he encourages them to abound in the knowledge of Christ so to grow in virtue and abound in the knowledge of Christ. The last part are verses 12 to 21, where he encourages them to pay attention to the prophetic word, which is the Old Testament.

St. Paul says, "Everything was written (he was referring to the Old Testament) for our teaching." Thus, the Old Testament or the prophetic word has a message to teach us and to help us. St. Peter is emphasizing, here, this same principle, that we need to pay attention to the prophetic word, because Christ is hidden in the Old Testament but is now revealed in the New Testament.

When you read the Old Testament, you need to search for Christ who is hidden—hidden in the prophesies, hidden in the characters, hidden in the types and symbols. In the Old Testament, Christ is hidden, but He is revealed in the New Testament.

Now that we have the whole Bible, both Old and New Testaments, we can understand the New Testament from the Old Testament and we can understand the Old Testament from the New Testament; both are very connected. For example, when you study the Letter to the Hebrews, you will find a strong connection between Hebrews and the Book of Leviticus; these two books are strongly connected to each other.

1:1 Simon Peter. In the first epistle, St. Peter refers to himself only as "Peter," but in this letter, he calls himself by both names: Simon Peter. As you know, Peter was the name given to him by the Lord Jesus Christ. When the Lord asked His disciples, "Who do men say that I, the Son of Man, am?" They replied, "Some say You are John the Baptist, some Elijah, some Jeremiah, one of the prophets" (Mt 16:13-14). But Simon told Him, "You are the Christ, the Son of the living God." Therefore, the Lord changed his name to Peter and told him, "You are Peter." Peter means small rock in Greek—Petros. However, the Lord Jesus used another word,

"Petra," which means faith. Thus, when the Lord said, "Upon this "rock" [Petra] I will build My church" (Mt 16:16-18), the Lord Jesus meant that He would build the Church upon this faith. This is an important distinction because the Roman Catholics confuse these two words.

Thus, the Lord used two different words: Petros and Petra. When He said, "I will build My church," He was saying He would build it upon petra, the huge rock, which is the rock of faith, but the name that was given to Peter was Petros.

For those who studied the anatomy of the skull, there is a small bone in the skull called the "petros bone." This bone is the strongest bone in the whole body. That is why they call it petros, which means "strong like a rock."

a bondservant and apostle of Jesus Christ. He describes his relationship with Christ on two levels: the first level, as a bondservant, and the second level, as an apostle. These are two dimensions. What is a bondservant and what is the difference between bondservant and a servant?

In the Jewish tradition, if a master has a servant, then on the seventh year he should release him. But if this servant goes to his master saying, "I love my master and want to remain with him," then, this servant, by his own free will and because of his love for his master,

chooses to serve him for the rest of his life (cf. Ex 21:5-6).

Therefore, this servant is not called a "servant" anymore, but is now called a "bondservant," because there is a bond, which is the bond of love that bonds him with his master. So, when St. Peter used the term "bondservant," he wanted to say, "I am not serving the Lord Jesus Christ out of obligation, I am not serving Him out of fear, but I am serving Him out of love. By my own free will, I choose to serve Him and be in this bond with Him, because I love Him. To serve him, this is the biggest blessing in my life." Before St. Peter described himself as an apostle, he described himself as a bondservant of the Lord Jesus Christ.

The second dimension is that St. Peter said, "I am an apostle." "Apostle" means carrying a message or epistle to deliver to people. Because the Lord asked the disciples to go and preach the good news of salvation and the good news of the gospel to people (cf. Mk 16:15), St. Peter is saying, "Now that I am an apostle, what I am writing to you are not my own words. This is the message that I am delivering to you from Christ. I am just a carrier of this message. I am a carrier of this epistle, but these words are not my words."

So, the word "apostle" gives him the authority to speak to us, and "bondservant" speaks of his personal relationship with Christ.

To those who have obtained like precious faith with us. What does he mean by "obtained like precious faith? As you know, in the first century, some people had seen the Lord Jesus Christ with their own eyes while others had not seen Him. St. Peter had previously told them, "Whom although you have not seen Him, yet you love Him" (cf. 1 Pet 1:8). Now, he is saying that those who had not seen Christ received equally the precious faith that those who saw Christ had received.

Those who had seen Christ and those who had not seen Christ with their own eyes, physically, they both received the precious faith—the faith that will save us. St. Peter says this because he is most likely speaking to people who were living or dispersed throughout Asia Minor; so, they probably had not seen Christ physically. Therefore, he says that although they did not see Him, they still obtained like precious faith with us. This saving faith, how did we receive it? He explains:

by the righteousness of our God and savior Jesus Christ. I want you to notice here that he describes Jesus Christ as "God and Savior." This verse proves the divinity of Jesus Christ. The Holy Spirit takes from the righteousness of Jesus Christ and gives to us. That is how we are saved. The only way to receive this precious faith is through the righteousness of the Lord Jesus Christ. The Lord Jesus Christ came to fulfill all righteousness,

as He had said to John the Baptist, "We ought to fulfill all righteousness" (cf. Mt 3:15). The righteousness of the Law that we could not fulfill, the Lord Jesus Christ fulfilled it on our behalf. Thus, He satisfied God's justice.

Now, His righteousness is reserved for us, and the Holy Spirit takes from His righteousness and gives to us when we believe in Him. The Holy Spirit gives us from the righteousness of Christ through certain channels. These channels are called the "Mysteries [Sacraments] of the Church," like in baptism, where we receive the righteousness of Christ and become children of God and are purified from our sins.

St. Peter is saying, "You obtained this precious faith, the faith that is able to save you, only by the righteousness of our God and Savior Jesus Christ. Through the righteousness of the Lord Jesus Christ, the justice of God is satisfied, and, this righteousness is now available for you to be righteous in Him."

1:2 **Grace and peace be multiplied to you in the knowledge of God and Jesus our Lord.** "Grace and peace" is the apostolic salutation. When you read the letters of St. Paul or the letters of St. Peter, they usually start their letters by saying "Grace and peace," or "Peace and grace." If you think about these two gifts, you will see that they are the most needed gifts in our lives. Without the grace of God, we cannot achieve anything, and that is why we need the grace of God, and it is the grace of the Holy Spirit. If God were to take away His grace from us, we would fail in everything we do. Without Him, we cannot achieve anything. In this world, there are many tribulations and hardships, and we need to have peace amid them, as the Lord said, "My peace I give to you, My peace I leave with you" (Jn 14:27). This is why all the apostles greeted people with "Grace and peace," and prayed that people would grow in peace and grace.

We, as parents, or as spiritual fathers, or Sunday School servants, need to pray for ourselves and for others that they may have peace and grace, as St. Peter said here, "Grace and peace be multiplied to you." He said grace before peace, because without the grace of God, you cannot have peace; without grace, there is no peace.

How do we obtain grace and peace? It is only obtained through the knowledge of God—through the knowledge of His Son Jesus Christ. When we speak about knowledge, we are speaking about experiential knowledge, not just knowing about Him but knowing Him. Knowing Him means to enter into a relationship with Him—with Christ. So, grace and peace come through the knowledge of God and of His Son Jesus Christ, and through our fellowship with

the Lord Jesus Christ.

1:3 as His divine power has given to us all things that pertain to life and godliness, through the knowledge of Him who called us by glory and virtue. St. Peter is saying that the divine power gives us everything we need in order to live godly lives, and that Christ's divine power has given us all things we need that pertains to life and godliness. Everything you need to live a godly life was given to you by His divine power. How? "Through the knowledge of Him [Jesus Christ]." When we know Him and when we are in fellowship with Him, we will have everything we need to live godly lives.

through the knowledge of Him who called us. God called us to live a godly life, and because He called us to godly and righteous lives, He gave us everything we need. That is why we do not have any excuse. God called us to live godly lives and provided us with everything we need to live godly lives, and this was given to us through the knowledge of Jesus Christ. This is what makes Christianity different from any other religion. Other religions are just a set of principles, do's and don'ts, morality, etc.; what you need to do. If you keep all the principles and morals given by the teachings of those religions, you will be saved, but this is a big lie because our morals and our works cannot save us; otherwise, Christ died for no reason.

Christianity is not a set of principles; yet, unfortunately, many people think of it as a set of principles: "We need to do this and not do that, do this and do not do this." That is why they stumble and struggle. Christianity is not a set of principles, but rather, Christianity is fellowship; it is a relationship with Christ.

Christ—God—came and became man for us to be united with Him, to enter into a relationship. Through this relationship, we are transformed from image to image, from glory to glory, until we are in His likeness. Similarly, when a person surrounds himself with a group of people, over time, he will become like them. If he surrounds himself with ungodly people, eventually, he will become ungodly like them, and if he surrounds himself with godly people, eventually, he will be like them. That is why St. Paul said, "Evil company corrupts good habits" (1 Cor 15:33).

When we enter into relationships with people, we should know that these relationships can change us. Do you not think that when you enter into a relationship with God Himself, that that relationship will not change you? This relationship will definitely transform you. Those who think of Christianity as a set of principles and just want to follow the moral code of Christianity, will stumble, struggle, and fail, because they cannot live up to these principles. But, if they enter into a relationship with Christ, into fellowship with Christ, through this knowledge, through this relationship, through this fellowship, they will be transformed, will bear the fruit of the Spirit within them, and will be in the likeness of His Son.

Thus, St. Peter is explaining to us how to live a godly life: Be in a relationship with Christ through the knowledge of Him. The divine power of God granted us all things we need to live a godly life. How do we receive these things? It is through the knowledge of God.
God called us to eternal glory. The end goal is to be glorified with Him. What is the way to be glorified with Him? It is to obtain Christian virtues.

by glory and virtue. Glory and virtue can be understood in two different ways. The first way is that He called us to eternal glory. That is the goal, the end; what are the means? It is by living a virtuous life. We can also understand it to mean that God called us by His glory and by His virtue. "By His glory," is because Jesus was glorified by offering Himself as a sacrifice on our behalf. Before His crucifixion, He said, "Father, glorify Your Son," (Jn 17:1) and in the Gospel according to St. John 7:39, we read that the Holy Spirit had not yet been given to them because Jesus was not yet glorified; He had not yet been crucified and ascended. Thus, He called us through His glory, through

His crucifixion, His incarnation, His resurrection, and His ascension. All this is the glory of Christ. The second way is by His virtue, which means righteousness. Through His fulfilling the righteousness of the Law on our behalf and keeping this righteousness for us as a resource, the Holy Spirit takes from His righteousness and gives to us.

1:4 by which have been given to us exceedingly great and precious promises. "By which" means by the glory and by the virtue of Christ. By His glorious acts (from incarnation to crucifixion, resurrection, ascension— all these glorious acts), and by His righteous life—by these two things we have been given exceedingly great and precious promises. The promise to be saved, the promise to be children of God, the promise to be part-heirs of the eternal kingdom, all these exceedingly great and precious promises were given to us by the glory and virtue of our Lord Jesus Christ.

that through these you may be partakers of the divine nature. "These," refers to the promises (through the promises that were given to us) that "you may be partakers of the divine nature." We know that if God promises, He will fulfill His promise. He promises that we will be partakers of the divine nature, definitely not partakers in the essence; nobody will be a partaker in

the essence of the divinity, but we will be partakers in the work of the divine nature. Thus, being renewed in the image of God is one of the promises we are given when we believe in the Lord Jesus Christ and are baptized; we are made a new creation.

When you are renewed in the image of God, when you have communion in Him like in Chrismation, the Holy Spirit abides in you and you in Him. When you dwell in God and God in you, now, you are a partaker with the divine nature, one with Him, the Holy Spirit abiding in you. You eat His body and drink His blood, so you are a partaker of Christ. "That through these you may be partakers of the divine nature."

having escaped the corruption that is in the world through lust. When you enter into a relationship with Christ and you become transformed into His image, this transformation will deliver you from the corruption in the world. All those who come to Christ and abide in Him have escaped from sin and corruption, having escaped the corruption that is in the world through lust.

Here, he tells us how our nature was corrupted: through lust. When Adam and Eve desired this forbidden tree— that is the lust that corrupted their nature. Now, with lust, the people who lust and desire ungodly things, this also leads them to corruption. But, those who come to Christ, into the real knowledge of Christ, they are transformed and they escape the corruption that is in the world through lust.

1:5 **But also for this very reason.** Which reason? He is telling you, "Now you know that God called you and promised you with all these exceedingly great and precious promises: to be children of God, to be heirs with Christ …" One of the promises that really surprised me is when the Lord Jesus Christ said, "He who overcomes will sit on My throne" (Rev 3:21). This is a very big promise, to sit on His throne, "Sit with Me on My throne." That is why St. Peter described these promises as great … exceedingly great promises. What do you need to do if you understand and comprehend these promises?

giving all diligence. You need to work diligently, to strive diligently, lest these promises will not be yours. It is like if you were to promise your son a precious gift, but he must do something in order to earn it; so, he must work diligently. I want to explain here that working in and of itself is not the price for these promises; rather, working shows our love to God and our commitment and dedication to live with Him. If a father were to say to his son, "If your grade point average is this or that, I will get you this car." The car is not the prize of the grade point average, but the grade point average shows the commitment of the son. That is why the father would give him the car. I do not want you to think that we earn the kingdom of heaven with our works. It is given to us as a free gift, but works are a condition because they show our faith, our commitment, and our devotion to live with Christ.

This verse is very, very important for those who deny the importance of works and say, "faith only counts." If it was by faith only and no works were required, St. Peter would not have said: "Giving all diligence," and then follow that with "you need to add," because to add means to work. "But also for this very reason [now knowing all these promises], giving all diligence [no exertion is to be spared; you need to do above and beyond all your effort; there must be the fullest cooperation with God\."

add to your faith virtue, to virtue knowledge. Then, St. Peter says that you need to act, but before we read this section, I want to first explain it to you. St. Peter mentioned eight things. The first of them is that you need to add virtue to your faith. Faith is the basis of our Christian life. You are not Christian if you do not believe that Jesus is God. Thus, the first step in our Christianity is to believe in Jesus, to believe that He is the Son of God, that He is the Savior of the whole world, to believe in His incarnation, crucifixion, resurrection, and ascension.

Just believing in Him is not enough,

as St. James said, "Even the demons believe" (Jam 2:19). That is why you need to add to your faith (which is the basis of Christian life); you need to add to it virtues. What are virtues? Virtues are Christian morals, the fruit of the Holy Spirit. This means you need to add work to your faith; otherwise, your faith will be like the faith of the demons. Therefore, you need to add.

When you add virtue, as St. Anthony the Great said, "Any virtue can be a vice (can turn into a vice), if we practice it without wisdom or without discernment." When we practice any virtue, we need to have wisdom and knowledge because virtues must be guided by knowledge; otherwise, they will run into zeal for God, but not according to knowledge, as St. Paul said in Romans 10:2 about the Jews, how they have zeal, but this zeal was not according to knowledge.

St. Peter is saying, "Here is your faith (the foundation), but to your faith you need to add virtue, but to your virtue, you need to add knowledge, because practicing virtue without knowledge can turn into a vice or into zeal for God, but not according to knowledge."
Then, he says that knowledge can turn into pride. That is why you need to deny yourself. How do you deny yourself? You deny yourself by denying your will and doing the will of God. To deny your will, you need to exercise self-control. What is Self-control? It is denying your own will. For example, when I am

fasting, that is denying my will; I will say, "No, I will not eat," and that is self-control. So, the more knowledge you have, the more you need to renounce and deny your own will. That is why he said, "You need to add to knowledge self-control." We can define Christian self-control as being the voluntary abstaining from all inward and outward pleasure, which does not lead to God. To abstain from all ungodly pleasures, whether inward or outward, that is self-control. Thus, St. Peter said that the foundation is faith, to that faith you need to add virtue, to virtue you need to add knowledge, and to knowledge you need to add self-control.

1:6 **to knowledge self-control.** Self-control is often not easy. Controlling oneself needs perseverance, it needs patience, needs bearing and forbearance—to bear and to forbear. To control yourself means to sustain your position and to abstain from ungodly pleasures, as we say in the Psali of Friday. You need to deny yourself daily and carry up your cross daily.

to self-control perseverance. As in fasting, we exercise perseverance to control ourselves. Also, in your chastity and in your purity, you need to control yourself and to exercise perseverance. Again, St. Peter says that faith is the foundation, and to faith you need to add virtue, to virtue you need to add knowledge, to knowledge you need to add self-control, and to self-control you need to add perseverance.

to perseverance godliness. Perseverance is the external form. You cannot persevere without having a godly heart from within you. That is why he said, "you need to add "to perseverance godliness," because this godliness is the proper support for perseverance. If you persevere but there is no inward godliness, you will not be patient and you will not be able to endure to the end, as the Lord said, "He who endures to the end will be saved." (Mt 24:13) Therefore, the only way to persevere and to endure to the end is to have a godly heart within you. That is why he said, "add to perseverance godliness." Thus, add to your faith, virtue, and to virtue add knowledge, to knowledge add self-control, to self-control add perseverance, and to perseverance you need to add godliness. Godliness and perseverance are a support system, like how they are usually found in the most successful addiction treatment programs, for example, the support groups of Alcoholics Anonymous. God created two beautiful support groups for us: our family and our church. These are the best support groups, as we pray in the Divine Liturgy, "He made us unto Himself an assembled people." In order to persevere and continue in perseverance, and in order to continue in godliness, you need support from others. That is why St. Peter said that you need to add godliness to perseverance, and brotherly kindness to godliness. "Self-

control" is needed because if a person is treated for alcoholism or addiction, he needs to exercise self-control, and self-control is better through support. That is why if I want to exercise self-control and live a godly life, I need to surround myself with godly people. Godly people will help with my godly life and will also help me with to persevere and to have self-control. That is why he said you need to add brotherly kindness to godliness.

1:7 to godliness. Godliness means the continual sense of God's presence in your life, to revere Him as a son reveres his own father, and to be confident in Him. It is the continual awareness of the presence of God in our lives, to revere Him and to have confidence in Him.

brotherly kindness. Godliness needs brotherly kindness, which will also appear and be manifested in our affection toward the brethren, and our natural affection and kindness will also be sanctified by godliness. When he said, "brotherly kindness," he was speaking about the relationship with our brothers and sisters in Christ. That is why he used the words, "brotherly kindness."

and to brotherly kindness love. You should not stop at this level (brotherly kindness). Rather, as a Christian, you need to grow from brotherly kindness to loving everyone, even your enemies.

That is why he said that you need to add to brotherly kindness love. Love is the heart element, the heart's affection that gives the brotherly kindness its power and sweetness. If brotherly kindness is for our brethren in Christ, then, love is for everyone, including our enemies.

The message that St. Peter is giving us is that you need to add. Do not be content with your current stature and say, "You know, that is enough." Growing is a sign of life. If you have a plant that does not grow, that means it is dead. That is why St. Peter is encouraging us to add to our faith.

Are we adding to our faith? Many people are forty, fifty, or sixty and they say, "We are beginners in our spiritual life." That means they do not add to their faith, but St. Peter is encouraging us to grow and to add.

I want you to understand the logic because understanding the logic will make it easier for you to remember these eight things: you need to add to your faith virtue, virtue needs knowledge and knowledge needs self-control, and self-control need perseverance and perseverance needs godliness, and godliness needs brotherly kindness and brotherly kindness needs love. These are the eight steps we need to add.

Again, we need to add virtue to faith, upon virtue you need knowledge, upon knowledge you need self-control, upon self-control you need perseverance, then you need to add godliness, brotherly kindness, and love.

1:8 For if these things are yours and abound, you will be neither barren nor unfruitful in the knowledge of our Lord Jesus Christ. If you have these eight points, if these eight points become yours and you are abounding in them, and growing in them, you will be neither barren nor unfruitful in the knowledge of our Lord Jesus Christ. Your knowledge of Christ will not be barren, will not be unfruitful, but you will bear the fruit of the Spirit in your life. "Every branch that does not bear fruit will be thrown away" (Jn 15:2).

Many people say, "We are Christian," but do you have fruit, or are you barren and unfruitful? If you are barren and unfruitful this means you are not adding to your faith. That is why St. Peter is telling us, "If these are yours and abounding in you, will never be barren, you will never be unfruitful in your knowledge of Jesus Christ."

If these qualities abound in you, you will be fruitful, showing that you have the knowledge of Christ, in reality. So, it will be a real fellowship—not just knowing about Him, but a real fellowship with Jesus Christ.

What about if you are lacking these eight

points? There is a very sad description of this that St. Peter gives in verse 9.

1:9 For he who lacks these things is shortsighted, even to blindness, and has forgotten that he was cleansed from his old sins. If you are lacking these eight points and are not adding, you are "shortsighted, even to blindness." Why shortsighted? Because you cannot see beyond the present time and cannot see toward eternity; you cannot see beyond our contemporary world.

After St. Peter said that such a person is shortsighted, he said, "No, actually, he is blind. He is blind and has forgotten that he was cleansed from his old sins." It is as if St. Peter is saying, "You came to Christ to cleanse you and you received these great promises, that you will inherit the kingdom of God, that you will sit on His throne, that you will be saved, that you will be children of God and heirs with Christ. So, did you forget all these promises? Why are you not adding to your faith? Why are you not growing? Why are you not multiplying and abounding in these qualities every day?"

Yes, this person is short-sighted even to blindness and has forgotten that he was cleansed from his sins. He who does not add these things to his faith is blind and cannot see God or His pardoning love. He has lost sight of the precious promises and cannot even see the relationship he once enjoyed with God. He forgot his purification from sins; otherwise, he would choose diligence lest he fall again into sin.

1:10 Therefore, brethren, be even more diligent to make your call and election sure. God called you, called you to all these precious promises, but if you are not diligent and if you are not adding, then, your calling and election will not be sure. That is why he said, "Brethren, be even more diligent to make your call and election sure." This is a response to Protestant theology, which says, once saved, always saved. If this was true, St. Peter would not have said, "Be even more diligent to make your call and election sure." Some people could be elected, but if they are not diligent and are not adding, they will lose their election. Thus, diligence to the end, endurance to the end, and perseverance to the end, are needed for salvation.

your call. St. Peter used the word "calling" before the word "election" because God calls everybody; everybody is called. Those who accept His calling, He elects and chooses them. Election comes when we accept God's calling, but the calling is for everyone, without exception. "Go and preach the gospel to the whole world," (Mk 16:15). Those who will accept the calling, they will be elected. That is why he said, "your call and election sure."

for if you do these things. This means that our own effort and work are needed to make our call and election sure. "If you do these things you will never stumble." If you add to your faith, daily, you shall never fail or fall. That is the importance of being diligent in adding to our faith every day.

you will never stumble. We stumble because we are not diligent. His Holiness Pope Shenouda III of thrice blessed memory used to say, "The main difference between saints and us is seriousness." They [the saints] took their spiritual lives seriously. They were diligent to add to their faith every day.

1:11 **for so an entrance will be supplied to you abundantly into the everlasting kingdom of our Lord and Savior Jesus Christ.** I hear many people say, "I just want to get into heaven, even to stand at the door," but St. Peter is saying, "No. Do you want to enter through a very, very big gate into the kingdom of heaven?" This is different than the wide gate here on earth. "An entrance will be supplied to you abundantly," means you will enter with confidence and with boldness into the everlasting kingdom.

We will be spiritually rich. We will enter in full victory to glory. That is what he

meant. An entrance, a big entrance, a big celebration will be supplied to you abundantly as you go into the everlasting kingdom, if you add the virtues mentioned above to your faith, then you will enter victoriously into the everlasting kingdom of our Lord and Savior Jesus Christ.

In 2 Corinthians, Chapter 3, St. Paul said that he had laid a foundation, and everyone was building upon this foundation. He was speaking about service and ministry. He said that some people will build gold and other people will build hay or wood. Then, fire would test each person's work. If it stands the fire, then that person will be saved, but if the fire burns their work, "If what I built was like hay or wood, I would lose my work."

St. Paul said, "But he will be saved as by fire" (1 Cor 3:15), which is like how when a person passes an exam just by 50 percent. There is a big difference between people who barely passed (saved as just by fire), versus people who are provided a big entrance; these people will be supplied a big entrance to the everlasting kingdom. Thus, St. Peter is telling you that if you add to your faith diligently, every day, then an abundant entrance will be supplied for you to enter the everlasting kingdom of our Lord and Savior Jesus Christ.

1:12 **For this reason I will not be**

negligent to remind you always of these things, though you know and are established in the present truth. St. Peter is saying, "Since these qualities are so necessary to your abundant entrance into Christ's kingdom (these eight points are very, very important), they are a must to enter abundantly into Christ's kingdom. So, I, as your apostle, as your shepherd, as your father, I will not be negligent to always remind you of these things." This is like a father who keeps reminding his son how important it is to study, how important it is to study, how important it is to study, so that the son will not just pass, but will graduate with honors. This shows the heart of St. Peter and it rebukes all of us, whether we are clergy or Sunday School servants or parents, because who among us is diligent in reminding his students or his children or his people all the time as to how they need to grow and add to their faith?

I will not. "I will not! I decided not to be negligent to remind you always, always, every day I will remind you of these things, so that though you know and are established in the present truth … although you know it, although you are established and confirmed in the truth of the gospel (that is why he said, "the present truth"), the truth that was revealed to us in the New Testament (the truth of salvation that is revealed to us in the New Testament), although I know that you know it and I know that you are established in this truth, but it is my responsibility to remind you all the time of these things."

1:13 Yes, I think it is right, as long as I am in this tent, to stir you up by reminding you. "Yes, I do not think I am doing something wrong. I have to do it this way, I have to remind you, and I think it is right [to do so] as long as I am in this tent, to stir you up by reminding you." Which tent? All the Church Fathers realized and acknowledged that they were sojourners here, strangers here. I like the word "sojourners" better because it means you are on a journey, going to heaven.

They knew they were sojourners; so, they considered their bodies as tents, because a person who is on a journey usually has a tent to move from place to place. Thus, he is saying, "As long as I am in this tent, as long as I am in the body (the tent he is referring to, here, is the present home of his spirit), as long as I am in this tent, it is right to remind you, to stir you up by reminding you, to motivate you and to encourage you." Again, we, as parents or clergy or Sunday school servants, must have the same spirit, to stir up others to grow and add to their faith daily.

1:14 knowing that shortly I must put off my tent, just as our Lord

Jesus Christ showed me. Putting off my tent means "I will die." So, knowing that shortly (very soon) I will die makes me more anxious to remind you to grow in your faith. Because, as I told you, in John 21:18-19, the Lord told St. Peter, "When you were young you girded yourself, but when you are old others will gird you." Thus, in the Holy Gospel according to St. John, he commented on this by saying that the Lord Jesus Christ referred to the type of death by which St. Peter would die. St. Peter, in fact, was martyred, crucified upside-down, and others did bind him to a cross and took him where he did not want.

St. Peter is saying, "Now I know that I will shortly die. I will be martyred as our Lord Jesus Christ had shown me." I want you to see, here, the peace that was in his heart, because if I knew that I would be dying very shortly, I might ask for the people's compassion or for their support. I would need people to encourage me or I would plead with the Lord to change the situation, but, here, St. Peter has peace in his heart. He is not concerned that he will die shortly, but rather, his main concern is to remind the people to grow; that is a real father. A real father, even when he approaches his own martyrdom, he becomes all the more zealous to remind people to grow in their faith.

1:15 **Moreover I will be careful to ensure that you always have a reminder of these things after my decease.** St. Peter is saying, "My responsibility to remind you will not end by my death. I want to make sure that even after I die, you will have a constant reminder to remind you that you need to add to your faith." His sincerity and his faithfulness are amazing! He cared about the people even after his death. It is almost 2,000 years after his death, after his martyrdom, and we still have this reminder (this epistle), and here we are, studying and reading together. St. Peter was careful to ensure that the people always would have a reminder and he succeeded. We have this reminder. This epistle is reminding us until now that we need to add to our faith. He admonished them, so that after his death they would remember his words by having this epistle with them. He cared about them, not only during his life, but even after his departure and his martyrdom.

1:16 **For we did not follow cunningly devised fables when we made known to you the power and coming of our Lord Jesus Christ, but were eyewitnesses of His majesty.** St. Peter is telling them that he wants them to take it very seriously, especially because he knows for sure that these teachings are not fables or human teachings. He is telling them, "There was no mistake or doubt about the gospel that we preached to you, no such fables as the mass of the Gentiles. We are not just making up stories and preaching to you. No, we did not follow cunningly devised fables (like the Gentiles) when we made known to you the power and coming of our Lord Jesus Christ. We preached to you the incarnation and coming of our Lord Jesus Christ and the divine power of salvation, how He saved us, and we were eyewitnesses of His majesty."

we ... were eyewitnesses of His majesty. He is now giving them evidence that the gospel that he is preaching to them is the true gospel. He said, "We were eyewitnesses." The most powerful witness is that of an eyewitness. He said, "I was there; I saw him. He told me to walk on the water and I did by His power. I saw Him heal so many people. I saw Him raise the daughter of Jairus. I saw Him call Lazarus out from the tomb four days after his death. I saw Him and His glory on the Mountain of Transfiguration (as we will explain later). I saw Him after His resurrection and we dialoged together. I was there when Thomas doubted His resurrection and the Lord told him 'Come and put your finger in the marks of the nails' (cf. Jn 20:27). I was with Him when He ascended and I saw how He was taken up in clouds to heaven. I was there when the Holy Spirit came upon us and we spoke in tongues and preached by the divine power, which came as He told us: 'Do not depart from Jerusalem until you receive power from on high' (Lk 24:49). Therefore, the power and coming of Jesus Christ, I know it. I was an eyewitness; we were eyewitnesses of His majesty."

Maybe, we are human beings bearing witness, but what about God the Father bearing witness to the Son? He did bear witness to the Son, at least three times: His baptism, His transfiguration, and before His crucifixion, "I have glorified and will glorify..." (Jn 12:28). Thus, when St. Peter said, "We are eyewitnesses of His majesty," he was referring to the instance of the Lord Christ's transfiguration.

1:17 **For He received from God the Father honor and glory when such a voice came to Him from the Excellent Glory: 'This is My beloved Son, in whom I am well pleased.'** Verse 17 speaks of the Holy Transfiguration, when the Lord took Peter, James, and John on a mountain and His face started to shine like the sun, and Moses and Elijah appeared there with Him. This is the second evidence. The first evidence is that they were eyewitnesses, the second evidence is that the Lord Jesus Christ received glory and honor from the Father; the Father honored and glorified Him. In this incidence, the Lord Jesus Christ only revealed part of His eternal glory. He showed them just a glimpse of His eternal glory, like a prophecy or a symbol or a first fruit of the glory that will be revealed when Christ comes again in His glory and the glory of His Father. God honored the Son and glorified Him by His [the Father's] declaration when He said, "This is My beloved Son." "He is My beloved because He obeyed Me, and in Him I am well pleased because He offered Himself as a sacrifice; listen to Him." This voice actually came twice: at His baptism (cf. Mt 3:17) and at His transfiguration (cf. Mt 17:5).

1:18 **And we heard this voice which came from heaven when we were with Him on the holy mountain.** Again, St. Peter is confirming, "I was there, with James and John," (James had already been martyred by the year A.D. 67. James, the son of Zebedee was martyred by Herod; but John was still alive). "And we heard this voice ["we" are James, John, and Peter] which came from heaven when we were with Him on the holy mountain [the Mount of Transfiguration]." Therefore, the first evidence is the eyewitness, the second evidence is the declaration from the Father, and the third evidence is in verse 19.

1:19 **And so we have the prophetic word confirmed.** What is the prophetic word? All the Old Testament, all the prophecies, these are all now confirmed.

When Isaiah said, "Behold, the virgin will conceive and give birth to a Son" (Is 7:14), this prophecy is now confirmed in Christ. Now, we have the prophetic word confirmed. Prophecies were sure words because they are the words of God, but they were fulfilled in Christ and became clearer in the Gospels and the New Testament. As I previously mentioned, Christ was hidden in the Old Testament but He is revealed in the New Testament. Thus, we have the prophetic word confirmed.

which you do well to heed. So many people say, "We do not read the Old Testament and we do not understand the Old Testament," although there are many commentaries available in the bookstores and on the Internet. There are many, many commentaries in Arabic and English, but some people still say they do not read the Old Testament. St. Peter is saying "you do well to heed," to listen, and to study the prophetic word. You need to study the prophetic word because Christ is hidden in the Old Testament, and as St. Paul also said, the Old Testament was written for our edification. Therefore, you need to heed these prophecies concerning Christ.

as a light that shines in a dark place. The Old Testament, before Christ, was like darkness—darkness because people were at enmity with God before salvation. However, these prophecies became like a lamp, a light shining in a dark place, a lamp shining in the darkness of the past giving light for a time before the morning star (the day star) arises, which is Jesus Christ.

until the day dawns and the morning star rises in your hearts. That is the day of the New Testament, the full light of the New Testament, and the morning star (referring to Jesus) arises, as we also read in Revelation 22:16. Thus, Jesus Christ, the Morning Star, is now shining in the world, but what if I am blind? Do you remember when St. Peter said, "He who is lacking these (eight) things is shortsighted even to blindness?" So, if I am blind, I will not see this light. If the light is shining at noontime, but I am blind, I cannot see it. That is why he said, "Until the morning star rises in your hearts." This is the true knowledge of Christ, that when you enter into this relationship with Him, Christ will be revealed in you. Christ will never be revealed in you unless you have this relationship with him, unless you add to your faith. By adding to your faith and by growing, Christ will be revealed in you. If my heart is dark, and if I am living in the darkness of blindness, when I study the Scripture—the Old and New Testaments, and when I enter into this real relationship with Christ, He will start shining inside my heart— "the morning star rises in your hearts."

1:20 knowing this first, that no prophecy of Scripture is of any private interpretation. Do not say that these writings are human writings, which they were written according to the knowledge, or feeling, or understanding of the prophets. These are the inspiration of the Holy Spirit and the evidence of that is that these prophecies were fulfilled. This is the fourth evidence. The first evidence is the evidence of the eyewitness, the second evidence is the declaration of the Father, the third evidence is the prophecies or the prophetic word, and the fourth evidence is the inspiration of the Holy Spirit. I want to emphasize a very important point here, that the Holy Spirit did not only inspire the prophets and authors to write, but until now, when we read the word of God, the grace and the power of the Holy Spirit accompanies every word. That is why St. Paul said, "The word of God is living, effective, sharper than a two-edged sword" (Heb 4:12). How? Because the Holy Spirit, until now, speaks to us through these words.

1:21 for prophecy never came by the will of man, but holy men of God spoke as they were moved by the Holy Spirit. Knowing this, I want you to be sure that when you read the Bible, you are not reading words of men, that no prophecy of Scripture is of any private interpretation, for prophecy never came by the will of man. Prophecies were not written according to the will and understanding of human beings, but according to the will of God.

but holy men of God spoke as they were moved by the Holy Spirit. "Moved by the Holy Spirit" means that the Holy Spirit inspired them, not that it dictated them. In other religions, inspiration is dictation, but in Christianity, the Holy Spirit does not dictate, as in, "Write, and I will dictate." No. The Holy Spirit moved them and protected them from making mistakes, taught them, reminded them, and protected them from any fallibility; that is the inspiration of the Holy Spirit. St. Peter is saying, "I want you to know that we have great promises. I want you to know that God gave us everything we need to live godly lives. I want you to know that the gospel that you received is the true gospel. We were eyewitnesses, the Father confirmed it, the Holy Spirit inspired the words, and we have the prophetic word fulfilled. For all these reasons, you need to grow. You need to be diligent to add to your faith. If you do not, you are shortsighted and blinded, but if you add to your faith, you will never stumble and there will be for you abundant entrance to the everlasting kingdom. You need to add to your faith virtue, to virtue knowledge, to knowledge self-control, to self-control perseverance, to perseverance godliness, to godliness brotherly kindness, and to brotherly kindness you need to add love. Therefore, if you have these things, you will never fail.

Chapter 1 Questions

1. In what way are grace and peace multiplied for the Christian?

2. What has God's divine power given to us? How?

3. What else has been given to us? Why?

4. What spiritual graces are we to diligently add to our faith?

5. What will be our condition if we abound in these graces?

6. What will be our condition if we lack these graces?

7. What benefit will there be in doing these things?

8. What was St. Peter careful to ensure concerning these things?

9. What did St. Peter hope to accomplish?

10. In making known the power and coming of the Lord Jesus, what did St. Peter claim?

11. What experience in Jesus's life does St. Peter refer to as an example of witnessing the Lord's honor?

12. In addition to apostolic testimony, what else do we have to which we should give careful heed?

13. What should be remembered regarding the prophetic word?

2

Chapter Outline

- Destructive doctrines (1-3)
- Doom of false teachers (4-11)
- Depravity of false teachers (12-17)
- Deceptions of false teachers (18-22)

Introduction

St. Peter concluded the first chapter by speaking about the prophetic word and how it was fulfilled and confirmed by the incarnation of the Son of God. However, as in the Old Testament, there were true prophets, and there were also false prophets. St. Peter is saying that there will be true and false prophets in every generation. As in the Old Testament, we had true prophets as well as false prophets, so in the New Testament, we also have true teachers and false teachers.

The focus of Chapter 2 is on false teachers. Beware of false teachers. What are the characteristics of false teachers? St. Peter said the characteristics of false teachers are the following:

(1) They deny the Lord who bought them (with His blood through His crucifixion) and secretly introduce destructive heresies. Denying the Lord means what? If they are preaching something other than what the Lord preached, they are denying the Lord. If they are giving a message other than what is given to us in Scripture, this is a denial of the Lord. When they introduce heretical teaching, this heretical teaching is a denial of the Lord, even if they claim to be Christian, like Arius did. When false teachers introduce heretical teaching, this heretical teaching is a denial of the Lord, even if they claim to be Christian, like Arius. Arius claimed to be Christian and was actually a priest in Alexandria, but he preached that Jesus is not equal to God, that He is an intermediate being between God and human beings. Thus, in introducing this heresy, he was denying God who bought him and died on the cross for him. St. Peter said that if these people (heretics) do not repent, they would be punished. That is why he said that God knows how to reserve the wicked for the day of punishment. This was a warning to them, that if they did not repent, they would be punished. Those who are godly, God will deliver them from temptation. Maybe some people will be deceived by the false teachings, but if you are seeking the truth and searching for God with all your heart, God will deliver you from temptation.

(2) These false teachers are very arrogant and very prideful. Because of their arrogance, they revile against authority, any type of authority, whether it is the authority of God or the authority of the Church or the authority

of dignitaries—any type of authority. They do not know how to submit.

(3) They are after money, which St. Peter refers to as "the wages of unrighteousness." In addition, he compared them to Balaam in the Old Testament, to whom they [false prophets] paid money to curse the people of God. Thus, St. Peter said that as Balaam with the wages of unrighteousness accepted to curse the people of God, false teachers are also after money, are greedy, are arrogant, and that is why they rebel and revile authorities.

(4) They promise good things, but they cannot deliver. That is why he described them as "wells without water," as when you see a well and assume there is water in it, but you find it empty when you try to retrieve water from it. "They are clouds with no rain." They give the impression that they will give you more freedom, more liberty, but in reality, they will lead you to more bondage and more slavery.

(5) In both their methods and promises, they seek to deceive others, even those who have escaped from the pollution of the world, those who repented and returned to God. Those who have escaped from the corruption of the world are those innocent people who will become the target of the false teachers. They want to deceive them.

As I have said several times, the power of Satan lies in his ability to deceive. Satan would be powerless if he lost his power to deceive. Like Satan, as his soldiers, the false teachers deceive people with their words. They deceive the simple and the innocent. By using deceitful methods and deceitful promises, they are able to tempt the simple and the innocent.

St. Peter concludes this chapter by saying that these false teachers are *enslaved* by the pollution and corruption of the world. Thus, their end will be worse than their beginning because they knew God and knew the way of righteousness. After knowing God, they rebelled against Him and are now teaching heresies. Furthermore, St. Peter said, "It would have been better for them if they had not known God altogether in the first place." This is the summary of the chapter and now we will study it verse by verse.

_____

2:1 But there were also false prophets among the people, even as there will be false teachers among you. As previously noted, St. Peter concluded Chapter 1 in verse 19 by speaking about the true prophets. Now he is about to speak about the false teachers. He says, "as among the people," meaning among the people of Israel. He is saying that as among the people of Israel, there were false prophets, so there will also be false teachers among you.

The term "false prophets" occurred several times in the Old Testament, for example in the Book of Jeremiah 5:31, 6:13, and 8:10—all these verses include references to false prophets. The Lord Jesus Christ also warned us against false prophets, as we read in Matthew 24:24.

Why do we call them "false teachers?" It is because they preach false doctrines. Not only did St. Peter warn us about false teachers, but St. Paul also warned against such false teachers, as in Acts 20:30.

They will cause division when they introduce heresies and heretical teachings, because some people will support them, and some people will be against them. This division is caused by false teachers.

That is why I can say that any heresy causes a schism, causes division in the Church—any heretical teaching. Let me tell you, Satan tried to divide and weaken the Church through persecution, but persecution never divided the Church. Persecution made the Church stronger and stronger.

Attacks from the outside never divided the Church. Therefore, Satan started to change his technique and began attacking the Church internally by stirring and moving false teachers to spread their heresies, like what happened with Arius, Nestorius, and Macedonius. The Church was never divided by persecution from outside, but it was divided by false teachers from within the Church. That is why a heresy is a schism or tends to produce a schism in the Church.

who will secretly bring in destructive heresies. Because they use deceptive methods, St. Peter said, "secretly bring in destructive heresies." From the outside, externally, they will look like true teachers, but they will interject and introduce their heresies in a secretive way to deceive others.

even denying the Lord who bought them. Some of them (some of the false teachers), like Arius, denied the divinity of Christ. They denied His atonement and His redemptive work, and this is considered as the peak or culmination of false teaching, like the Jehovah Witnesses who deny the divinity of the Lord Jesus Christ, like the Mormons who deny the divinity of the Lord Jesus Christ, although they claim to be Christians, but they deny the Lord who bought them, "even denying the Lord who bought them."

and bring on themselves swift destruction. The Lord said, "Offences will come, but woe to him who brings in offences; it is better for him to be drowned in the sea" (cf. Mt 18:7). Because these false teachers divide the Church, their destruction and punishment will be severe. St. Peter used the word "swift" which means quick and sudden destruction.

2:2 And many will follow their destructive ways, because of whom the way of truth will be blasphemed Unfortunately, many people will follow them. These false teachers will have many followers. That is why you cannot judge a teacher by how many follow him. They said that Arius was a very eloquent speaker and that he composed many songs, but he used his talents to deceive people. Church historians have said that unless God had protected Athanasius, the whole world would have become Arians. Therefore, do not judge a teacher by how many are following him. St. Peter said that many will follow their destructive ways.

Not only that, but those who follow the truth and defend it will be blasphemed by them (the false teachers). Because they will be standing against these false teachers, these people will be attacked, and the false teachers and their followers will blaspheme the way of truth. The way of truth will be evil-spoken-of. They will speak evil about those who are defending the truth and the way of the truth. Because false teachers blend the false teaching with the true teaching together, they blaspheme the way of righteousness and the way of truth.

2:3 By covetousness they will exploit you with deceptive words; They use deception to exploit you (to use you). False teachers will use the simple people, the innocent people, and will exploit them by deceptive words. What is their motive? It is greed, love of money, and covetousness. Thus, covetousness is the companion of a heresy.

The false teachers use souls. They use the simple people to gain by them, as merchants use their words. But the gain here is not necessarily a financial gain. Some people are after fame. They want to have a name. They want to have a reputation. They want to have popularity. These are all considered gain. Gain is not only financial gain, but can be in the form of popularity, fame, reputation, etc. St. Peter is warning us, lest if we are unwise, they will exploit us and use us by covetousness and deceptive words. "Deceit is the tool they are using to exploit you."

for a long time their judgment has not been idle, and their destruction does not slumber. Those who will cause division in the Church by false teaching, God will execute judgment speedily upon them. "For a long time their judgment has not been idle, and their destruction does not slumber," which means that God will speedily execute His judgment upon them.

All sinners will be judged to destruction, and God's punishment of some proves He will judge the rest. If God judged the fallen angels, then, this is a proof and evidence that these false teachers will not escape the judgment of God.

The Coptic Synaxarion reveals that when Pope Archelaus did not listen to his spiritual father, Pope Peter I (known as the last martyr or the seal of the martyrs), and accepted Arius in the Church and ordained him a deacon, he did not stay on the throne of St. Mark for more than six months. Because he (Pope Archelaous) did not listen to his spiritual father, Arius deceived him; and Pope Archelaous accepted him in the Church and ordained him a deacon.

In verse 4, St. Peter gives us several examples of how God did not spare the fallen angels, the wicked and the bad people from judgment. Thus, he is saying, "As God did not spare any of these people, in the same way, He will not spare any false teachers."

2:4 **For if God did not spare the angels who sinned, but cast them down to hell and delivered them into chains of darkness, to be reserved for judgment.** He is now speaking about the fallen angels. To prove that the judgments on these wicked, false teachers, are sure, St. Peter starts talking about the fallen angels who sinned, saying that they

were cast out of heaven. In this verse, the word "hell," translated from Greek is not "Gehenna" or "Gehinnom" but in Greek the word used is "Tartarus," which is a term used to refer to a place in which beings await future punishment; thus, it refers to Hades. As we read in the Book of Revelation, in the Second Coming of Christ the Lord, He will cast down Satan into Gehenna or Gehinnom, which is the lake of fire, but until now, they (the angels who sinned) are not there; they are in Hades (a waiting place—a place for future punishment). The fallen angels became angels of darkness bound with chains and excluded from the light of heaven. They are not in heaven anymore nor are they enjoying the light of heaven.

to be reserved for judgment. They say that Satan is bound by chains, so how is he able to do all this wickedness in the world? If you bind or hold a dog with a chain, the dog can still move freely, as far as the chain will allow him to move. In the same way, if chains bind Satan, he can still move freely within that limit. Of course, the chains are not physical chains, but this shows that God has set boundaries for them (Satan's angels—demons), where they can or cannot go, what they can do, and what they cannot do. Thus, when we say that Satan is bound by chains, it means his power is limited and there are boundaries on him; he cannot do whatever he wants to do. These chains do not hinder their Satan and the fallen angels from walking to and fro and seeking those whom they may devour (cf. Job 1:6–12), but they are restricted in their freedom; they do not have absolute freedom. Nonetheless, at the end of the days, Satan will be loosed from these chains and this will be the time of the Great Tribulation.

they did not listen to him. He was a preacher of righteousness by example because he lived a righteous life, and also by his words; but, unfortunately, these ungodly people did not listen to him. The third example is Sodom and Gomorrah, in verse 6.

2:5 and did not spare the ancient world, but saved Noah, one of eight people. St. Peter is giving us another example. The first example was the example of the fallen angels. The ancient world is the world during the time of Noah and in the Ark, and the eight people that were saved: Noah, his wife, his three sons (Shem, Ham, and Japheth) and each son's wife. Eight persons only were saved in the Ark.

a preacher of righteousness, bringing in the flood on the world of the ungodly. The case of the ancient world is the second example of God's swift justice. God did not flood everybody. He delivered the righteous Noah and his family. God did not forget His righteous people, Noah and his family, but He asked them to build an ark to save them. During the time of the building of the Ark, which took 120 years, Noah was preaching righteousness. That is why St. Peter described him as a "preacher of righteousness." He called people to repent, to live a righteous life, and to enter into the Ark with him, but

2:6 and turning the cities of Sodom and Gomorrah into ashes, condemned them to destruction, making them an example to those who afterward would live ungodly. The main sin of Sodom and Gomorrah was the sin of homosexuality. That is why the word "sodomy" is used to refer to homosexuality. When you read the word "sodomy," it is a reference to homosexuality. Why? It is because the main sin of Sodom was homosexuality. Thus, the following generations until now still refer to homosexuality as "sodomy."

God turned the cities of Sodom and Gomorrah into ashes because they did not repent; they did not listen to Him. He made them an example to those who live ungodly. The message here to the false teachers is that if God did not spare the fallen angels, nor the ancient world, nor Sodom and Gomorrah, but condemned them [all] to destruction, God will also not spare the false teachers.

However, as I told you, God saves His

people. If there is one righteous person, if there are three righteous people, God will save them. He saved Noah, one of eight, from the flood of the ancient world, and He also saved Lot and his two daughters from Sodom and Gomorrah, as we read in verse 7.

2:7 **and delivered righteous Lot, who was oppressed by the filthy conduct of the wicked.** Living among the wicked and living among the ungodly will tempt you to be ungodly like them. If you try to resist and hold on to your righteousness, you will be torturing your soul every day; you will be oppressed by the filthy conduct of the ungodly. This was the case of Lot who lived among the wicked people of Sodom and Gomorrah. He was oppressed by their filthy conduct, as St. Peter said. Lot was torturing himself by what he was seeing and hearing every day, but God saved Lot the righteous from the destruction of Sodom and Gomorrah.

Why did St. Peter call the people of Sodom and Gomorrah "wicked?" It is because they rebelled against the Law of God, the law of man, and the law of nature. Homosexuality is against the Law of God. God created Adam and Eve—a man and a woman. He did not create two men or two women. God's purpose for marriage is for it to be a relationship between a man and a woman.

It is against the law of men, because even for those who do not know God, marriage for them is between a man and a woman. It is also against the law of nature because the anatomy or physiology of the body is against homosexuality. That is why he said that these wicked people are against the Law of God, the law of man, and the law of nature.

2:8 **(for that righteous man, dwelling among them, tormented his righteous soul from day to day by seeing and hearing their lawless deeds).** That is why St. Paul in his second letter to the Corinthians said, "There is no fellowship between darkness and light. There is no fellowship between the children of God and the children of Belial" (cf. 2 Cor 6:14). Be separate from them; do not dwell among ungodly people. St. Paul also said that "bad company corrupts good morals" (cf. 1 Cor 15:33). Thus, you need to separate yourselves from ungodly people. We have the example of Lot, how he tormented his righteous soul from day to day by seeing and hearing their lawless deeds. He had a troubled soul. His soul was troubled because every day he witnessed their lawlessness and was grieved; so, he lived a painful life.

2:9 then the Lord knows how to deliver the godly out of temptations and to reserve the unjust under punishment for the day of judgment. Here, he is giving us a message of hope, that even if you are living in a world that is full of wickedness, full of lawlessness, and full of ungodliness, if you hold onto your righteousness, God will save you as He saved Noah and as He saved Lot. These examples show that the Lord knows how to deliver the righteous from trials. This example also shows that God will reserve the unjust and the wicked and the ungodly to the Day of Judgment to be punished. Therefore, it is your choice either to live a righteous life and God will deliver you, or to choose the way of wickedness and be among the people who will be judged and punished on Judgment Day.

2:10 and especially those who walk according to the flesh in the lust of uncleanness and despise authority. He is talking here about the carnal people, those who satisfy the lust of the flesh, and who are led by the desires of the flesh and not by the Spirit of God. Thus, the people who will receive the greater punishment are: 1) False teachers because they divide the Church of God. 2) Carnal and the impure people because they defile the temple of God, as St. Paul said, "You are the temple of God and the Holy Spirit abides in you" (cf. 1 Cor 3:16, 6:19). He who destroys the temple of God, which is your body, God will destroy him. 3) The rebellious because they rebel against authorities. Why? If you rebel against authority, you will eventually rebel against the authority of God. That is why he said, "and especially those who walk according to the flesh in the lust of uncleanness and despise authority;" They refuse to submit to any authority. What is the sin of the fallen angel? What is the sin of Satan? He refused to submit to the authority of God. That is arrogance. That is pride. False teachers usually do not submit to authority and they are tempted by uncleanness and carnal sins.

They are presumptuous, self-willed. They are not afraid to speak evil of dignitaries. In verse 10, St. Peter begins to describe those who are carnal. One characteristic is their arrogance and stubbornness; they are stubborn. Those who do not submit are arrogant and stubborn. Not only do they not submit, but also, they are not afraid to speak evil of persons in authority. Although they are insignificant in their power and in their might, but because of their arrogance, they are not afraid to speak evil of persons in authority.

We see nowadays how people are unafraid to speak evil of the authorities; for example, unfortunately, some people say negative things about His Holiness. St. Peter is warning us: "This is arrogance, this is stubbornness, and these people will receive greater punishment."

That is why he described them as "presumptuous and self-willed." They do not put their will under the will of God, but they execute their own will— self-will. Instead of saying, "Thy will be done," they say, "my will be done," and they are not afraid to speak evil of dignitaries.

He said, the angels (not the fallen angels but the godly angels) respect people in authority and they do not speak evil about people in authority. Do you remember when St. Paul was on trial and he spoke negatively to the high priest who was testing him? When they asked him, "Did you know that that is the high priest?" he replied, "I did not know, brethren, that he was the high priest; for it is written, 'You shall not speak evil of a ruler of your people'" (cf. Acts 23:5; Ex. 22:28; Eccl. 10:20; 2 Pet. 2:10.).

St. Peter is giving us a very nice example here (in verse 11), that the angels—even the angels, do not speak negatively about people in authority.

2:11 **whereas angels, who are greater in power and might.** It is definite that angels are superior in their power and might—greater than us.

do not bring a reviling accusation against them before the Lord. "Them," here, refers to the dignitaries, to those who are before the Lord. The angels who are superior in might and power do not show such disrespect to the people in authority; yet, these arrogant false teachers speak negatively about people in authority. In this part of the chapter, St. Peter tells us that the false teachers, the carnal people, and the rebellious people will receive greater punishment, and they should repent because if they think God will spare them, they are deceived. God did not spare the fallen angels, He did not spare the ancient world, and He did not spare Sodom and Gomorrah.

2:12 **But these, like natural brute beasts made to be caught and destroyed, speak evil of the things they do not understand, and will utterly perish in their own corruption.** He is saying that beasts are caught to be killed; and these people—the false teachers, the carnal people, and the rebellious people—are like these beasts. When they speak irrationally, when they revile against God and against those in authority, they hand themselves over to destruction, to be caught by God and destroyed in the lake of fire. Likewise, when these teachers speak of things they do not understand, what will happen to them? They "… will utterly perish in their own corruption." Thus, these men are willingly casting themselves into Satan's snares to be destroyed. As animals are caught, Satan is catching them; thus, they are destined to be slaughtered.

2:13 and will receive the wages of unrighteousness, as those who count it pleasure to carouse in the daytime. These people speak evil of things they do not understand. False teachers do not understand the truth of the Gospel. That is why they introduce false doctrines or speak of angels or of heavenly things, or they speak of God things they do not understand. They speak negatively about Him.

Their own wicked conduct will bring them to destruction, and eternal punishment will be the wage of their unrighteousness. That is why St. Peter said they "will receive the wages of unrighteousness." What are the wages of sin? Death. The wages of unrighteousness are eternal punishment. The wages of sin is death and the wages of unrighteousness is eternal punishment. St. Peter tells us, "Do you know how they are irrational? I will give you an example of how they are irrational: They lose their eternal life for the pleasure of one day. A carnal man who is following the lust of the flesh may lose his eternal glory for the pleasure of a moment or the pleasure of one day." That is why he said, "those who count it pleasure to carouse in the daytime"—to celebrate

in ungodly ways or engage in ungodly entertainment or ungodly fun. They are forgetful of the coming destruction and they take pleasure in carousal for a day, regardless of the morrow, regardless of their eternal life.

They are spots and blemishes. That is why St. Peter said, "They are spots and blemishes." It is as if you have clean clothes and some spots come on them. How will these spots disfigure or mess up your clothes? In the same way, these people in the midst of the Church, the false teachers or the carnal people or the rebellious people, St. Peter is describing them as spots and blemishes in the Church of God, disfiguring the beauty of the Church.

carousing in their own deceptions. They take pleasure in their own sins and lusts, by which they deceive others. They deceive others by their own sins and lusts in which they are taking pleasure.

while they feast with you. This refers to their celebrating the Eucharist or any other activity with us. They are like spots and blemishes while they are celebrating and feasting with us.

2:14 having eyes full of adultery and that cannot cease from sin. The carnal man's entire mind and heart are full of the lust of the flesh. That is why he looks around with a lustful appetite and his eyes cannot cease from sin, all the time. Even when he sees something good, he looks at it in a lustful way. His eyes cannot stop nor cease from sin.

enticing unstable souls. Simple people, those who are unstable, those who are not firmly established in their faith, in their piety, and in their spiritual lives, they will be easily deceived and easily enticed by the carnal people, the false teachers, and the rebellious people. That is why you need to be confirmed in your faith. You need to be confirmed in your piety and in your righteousness; otherwise, you will be enticed and seduced by these people because they entice unstable souls.

They have a heart trained in covetous practices, and are accursed children. Be careful. They are very, very well trained in covetous practices. They know how to deceive others and how to exploit others. Not only are their eyes full of adultery, but also their hearts, because the heart is the fountainhead of lust and from the heart comes adultery to the eyes. It starts in here, within the heart, and then goes to your eyes. These people, because they are trained in covetous practices— knowing how to deceive others, how to exploit others, and how to gain from others, are not blessed but are accursed children. They will be cursed by their conduct and behavior. Cursing and covetousness go hand in hand. St. Peter will give us the example of Balaam

from the Book of Numbers (22:15).

2:15 They have forsaken the right way and gone astray, following the way of Balaam the son of Beor. Balaam was a prophet and the king of Moab gave him money to curse the people of Israel. He was riding his donkey on the way to Moab when the Angel of God appeared and stopped the donkey from going to Moab. The donkey saw the Angel of God, but Balaam did not see Him. Balaam began to beat the donkey, but the donkey could not move because the Angel was standing before him; so, the donkey smashed his leg against the wall. God gave power to the donkey to speak, and the donkey rebuked Balaam. When Balaam arrived, he could not curse the people of Israel, but he blessed them against his own will because prophecy comes by the inspiration of the Holy Spirit. Thus, he said to the king, "I cannot curse the people whom God has blessed" (Num 23:8). Then, he proposed very bad counsel to the king. He told him, "Do you want the children of Israel to be accursed? Let me tell you how: Send the women or the females of Moab to seduce the men of Israel, to make them fall into adultery with them. Once the people fall into adultery, God will leave them. When God leaves them, you can defeat them; you can overpower them." That is what happened.   That is why St. Peter said that these false teachers, these carnal people who entice others to sin and to lust, these rebellious people, have forgotten the right way, the way of righteousness, and have gone astray, gone after the lust of the flesh, gone after their own will and their own minds, in stubbornness and rebellion.

who loved the wages of unrighteousnes. That is to say, he loved the greed and money of unrighteousness. Balaam sold himself out to an evil cause for the sake of gain.

2:16 **but he was rebuked for his iniquity: a dumb donkey speaking with a man's voice restrained the madness of the prophet.** This prophet (Balaam) became mad; he lost his mind. Who rebuked him? Who restrained him? A dumb donkey speaking with a man's voice restrained the madness of this prophet. The donkey that he rode rebuked him. You can find this story in Numbers, Chapter 22, where God made the donkey to speak to rebuke this prophet.

2:17 **These.** "These" refers to the false teachers, to the carnal, and to the rebellious people. Usually, these three things are in one person.

are wells without water. They promise much but they cannot fulfill their promises. They disappoint, like a well that promises you water, but there is no water in it.

clouds carried by a tempest. As clouds carried by tempests promise rain, but they fail to descend water, so these false teachers promise you liberty and salvation; but on the contrary, they are wells without water and clouds carried by a tempest.

for whom is reserved the blackness of darkness forever. For these rebellious leaders, the blackness of darkness is reserved; but, what does "the blackness of darkness" mean? It means the severest punishment in hell, the eternal separation from the presence of God and from the glory of His power. Therefore, we can say that false and corrupt teachers will be sent to the lowest hell. That is why St. Peter said that the blackness of darkness is reserved for them, forever.

2:18 **For when they speak great swelling words of emptiness.** St. Peter is saying that they speak great swelling words of emptiness; their words are deceptive. "Great swelling words" means very powerful words, but when you think about what they are saying, they are nothing. They are not saying anything; they are empty words. They promise great things, but they disappoint; they cannot fulfill their promises. Great swelling words but are empty, big words but nothing in them. They say big, big words, but there is nothing in them.

they allure through the lusts of the flesh, through lewdness. They deceive and entice through the lusts of the flesh. They will tell you that you can do whatever you want to do, like those who are preaching homosexuality. Some churches approve of homosexuality, so they are enticing people through the lusts of the flesh—through lewdness. They approve drinking, dancing, sexual immorality and say that God is not against these activities.

the ones who have actually escaped from those who live in error. Through the lusts of the flesh and through lewdness, they entice "the ones who have actually escaped from those who live in error." They entice simple people who have already repented and escaped from the people who are living in error, but they bring them back to an ungodly life. They entice those who have been delivered from the company of them who live in error. How? They use lust and profanity. They are not only false teachers, but they also deceive people. They deceive people who have already repented and they bring them back to wickedness.

2:19 While they promise them liberty. "Liberty, freedom, do whatever you want to do; there are no restraints. If you want to live in homosexuality, go ahead, do it. Sexual immorality? There is nothing wrong with it. Drinking, dancing? Nothing wrong with that." Liberty from all restraint, complete freedom to serve their own wills against the Law of God, they promise freedom from any restrictions, "Do whatever you want to do; make your own law." They encourage complete freedom from the will of God, allowing you to serve your own desires and your own lusts.

they themselves are slaves of corruption. Thus, they are promising liberty, not realizing that they are enslaving people to these bad habits. Those who offer liberty are themselves slaves to these habits. They are slaves to drinking, they are slaves to alcohol, they are slaves to homosexuality. They are slaves serving their own passions and lusts. They themselves are slaves of corruption.

for by whom a person is overcome, by him also he is brought into bondage. St. Peter is telling us a very important rule here—a golden rule that I want you to understand very well. He is saying that if a certain habit is overcoming you, you are under bondage to this habit. So, if alcohol has overcome you, you are not free; you are a slave to alcoholism. If gambling overcomes you, you are a slave to that habit. If sexual immorality overcomes you, you are a slave to that habit, etc. Therefore, by any habit that a person is overcome, "by it (that bad habit) also he is brought into bondage." You are under bondage; you are not free.

2:20 For if, after they have escaped the pollutions of the world through the knowledge of the Lord and Savior Jesus Christ, they are again entangled in them and overcome, the latter end is worse for them than the beginning. St. Peter is saying, "If you have already escaped corruption (you know Jesus Christ, and through this knowledge, you have escaped from the corruption and pollution of the world) then, you return (you relapse to your former life), the end will be worse than the beginning. If one who has been converted and repented is enticed back again to his former sin, his end is worse than the former. Why is that? A relapse (the Biblical term for relapse is apostasy, which means falling back, or returning—the apostasy) is more inexcusable because you already tasted Christ. If you had not tasted Christ, you may have an excuse; but if you tasted Christ, then rebel against Him. This is inexcusable, and this will cause greater condemnation. That is why he said, "The latter end is worse for them than the beginning."

2:21 For it would have been better for them not to have known the way of righteousness, than having known it, to turn from the holy commandment delivered to them. St. Peter is saying, "It would have been better for them if they had not known the way of righteousness, but now they know it and rebel against it. This has made their case worse because they add the sin of rejecting the way of righteousness after having knowledge to their other sins." For example, they have now added another sin on top of the sin of immorality, the sin of lewdness, and the sin of covetousness, which is the sin of rejecting the way of righteousness after having known and experienced the Lord Jesus Christ.

2:22 But it has happened to them according to the true proverb: 'A dog returns to his own vomit,' and, 'a sow, having washed, to her wallowing in the mire.' A dog, after he vomits, goes back to his vomit to eat it. So, these people, after they vomited their sins and repented, they return to their vomit (their former sins) and live a sinful life again. This relapse, this apostasy, is described in Proverbs 26:11. This repulsive course can be compared to the most disgusting habits of unclean animals, that just as a dog vomits and returns and eats his vomit again, so you go back to these sins and eat them again. Also, as swine, having washed, go back wallowing in the mire, so after you are cleansed, after the Lord Jesus Christ cleansed you from your sins, you go back wallowing yourself in the mire of sin. Thus, this is the chapter in which St. Peter is warning us of false teachers, carnal people, and the rebellious, telling us that these people will receive a greater damnation. However, God will save the righteous from among them and from temptation and trial.

Chapter 2 Questions

1. What is meant by false prophets?

2. What impact can their teaching have on their followers?

3. What are the two main sins of heretics? (v.10)

4. In verses 15–16, there is mention of Balaam. Who is he and what was his main problem?

5. The last paragraph talks about the false meaning of liberty. Please explain.

3

Chapter Outline

- God's promise is not slack (1-9)
- The day of the Lord (10-13)
- Be steadfast (14-18)

Introduction

In this chapter, St. Peter is reminding us to pay attention to the words of the apostles that were recorded in the Old Testament, the words of the apostles that were recorded in the New Testament, and also to the words of our Lord Jesus Christ, especially as some false teachers and scoffers would cast doubts in the hearts of the people, making them doubt the word of God regarding His Second Coming—His promise to come to the world, to judge it, and to take His beloved and chosen ones to the kingdom of heaven.

St. Peter analyzed and responded to their accusations that nothing is happening and that the Lord is delayed by saying that this delay is an indication of the Lord's longsuffering and patience. He is giving us a chance to repent.

St. Peter also reminded them how during the time of the flood (cf. Genesis 6–9) the longsuffering of God was demonstrated as He waited for 120 years! The people did not pay attention and thought that God forgot His warning, until the day of the flood came and flooded the world.

St. Peter tells them that the day of the Lord will come as a thief, unexpected, and that is why we, as Christians, need to focus on holy conduct and godliness. The longsuffering of the Lord is an opportunity for us to work on our salvation.

He also mentioned to them that this doctrine is not his teaching but it is the teaching of all the apostles, as they received from the Lord Jesus Christ. He told them that even St. Paul wrote the same things about the Second Coming of the Lord.

St. Peter concluded with this chapter, which is the last chapter of this epistle, and also his conclusion of the whole epistle, by instructing us with admonitions to beware lest we fall and asking us to grow in the grace and knowledge of the Lord Jesus Christ. He concludes with a doxology, or glorification, to Christ. This is the summary of the chapter. Now, let us read it verse by verse.

3:1 Beloved, I now write to you this second epistle (in both of which

I stir up your pure minds by way of reminder). Because he said, "I write to you this second epistle," this language implies that the First Epistle of St. Peter was written to the same people to whom the second epistle also addresses. Thus, he addressed both letters to the same people, and he is telling them, "My objective in both letters is to remind you, to stir up your pure minds as to how to live a holy life." His main objective was to exhort them to holy lives.

3:2 **that you may be mindful of the words which were spoken before by the holy prophets and of the commandment of us, the apostles of the Lord and Savior.** "I am reminding you," St. Peter is saying, "of the Christian teaching, as shown by the prophets and the apostles. These words of the prophets and apostles are the words of God, because the prophets were sent by God and the apostles are messengers of God." Thus, the words of the prophets and words of the apostles are authoritative because they are the words of God. Therefore, St. Peter is telling them, "I want you to pay attention to what is written by the prophets in the Old Testament, and also what is written in the New Testament by us, the apostles of our Lord and Savior Jesus Christ."

3:3 **knowing this first: that scoffers will come in the last day, walking according to their own lusts.** St. Peter is telling them, "As we have true teachers like the prophets and the apostles, in every generation, there will also be false teachers and false prophets, but the number of the false teachers will increase greatly in the last days." Therefore, when we see today many denominations and many teachers teaching in the name of Christ but they do not teach the truth of the Scripture, this will be a sign of the end of days.

St. Peter said that these teachers are not moved by the Holy Spirit but are inspired by "their own lusts." They are inspired by their own desires, by their own indulgences. A true teacher is inspired and moved by the Holy Spirit, but a false teacher is inspired and moved by his own personal lusts, desires, and indulgences. Such people (false teachers), instead of confirming your faith, they cast doubt on your faith. That is why St. Peter called them, "scoffers."

3:4 **and saying, "Where is the promise of His coming? For since the fathers fell asleep, all things continue as they were from the beginning of creation."** It is the scoffers asking the question in verse 4 and casting doubt on the promises of God. God promised that He will come again, but they are saying His coming is delayed and they do not know for sure whether He is coming or not. Thus, all hope had ended. They (the scoffers) take advantage of the delay of the Lord and destroy the faith of the people. They say, "You know, from our fathers, as in from the beginning of time or from the beginning of creation, everything is the same. The regular order of things continues on as it was from the beginning. Everything is the same from the time of Adam until now, so we do not have any indication that the Lord is coming again."

3:5 For this they willfully forget. "Willfully" means intentionally. They have intentionally forgotten things that have happened in the world (speaking about the flood). St. Peter is saying that if they consider the flood, they would not say this. Why the flood?

that by the Word of God, the heavens were of old. So, he says to them, "How did God create the world? He created it by His Word. These heavens were created by the Word of God."

and the earth standing out of water and in the water. What does this statement mean? It means that water is the principle element in its formation. It is a scientific fact that three-fourths of the surface of the earth are seas and oceans (water). Thus, the earth is standing out of the water; that is true.

Water is also found in the depths of the earth—everywhere. When we dig inside the earth, we reach a level of deep waters. Water is on the surface of the earth and deep down in the earth. St. Peter is saying, "By His Word, God created everything, and by the means of water, He created heaven and earth." I also want to remind you that in Genesis, Chapter 1, God created the firmament, and the firmament spread between water above the firmament and water under the firmament. Water above the firmament is clouds, and this is considered as the first heaven. So, heaven and earth are made of water— "by the Word of God." The same Word that created heaven and earth and formed them from water, the same Word used the water to flood the world when the windows of heaven were opened, and the old world was overthrown and perished with water.

3:6 by which the world that then existed perished, being flooded with water. This same Word of God that created and founded and formed heaven and earth from water, this same Word also destroyed the whole earth during the time of Noah by the flood, and this was against nature and against the law of nature. St. Peter is asking, "Why do you forget this? Why do you willfully forget this? Because the same Word that is preserving heaven and earth until this day, this same Word will also destroy heaven and earth in the Second Coming of the Lord."

3:7 **But the heaven and the earth which are now preserved by the same Word are reserved for fire until the day of judgment and perdition of ungodly men.** The "same Word" means the Word of God. He is saying that the same Word that created the heaven and earth out of water is the same Word that flooded the world by water. The same Word of God that preserves heaven and earth until now is the same Word that will also destroy heaven and earth in the Second Coming of the Lord, in which He will come to judge the world, and the ungodly people will perish on that day. St. Peter is saying that the same Word of God has always been shown, and as the prophets and apostles declared to us that Word, which is what has kept the earth and heaven reserved for fire (and this will happen), this is the same Word of God. This destruction by fire will happen when the Lord comes and when perdition comes on ungodly men.

3:8 **But, beloved, do not forget this one thing, that with the Lord one day is as a thousand years, and a thousand years as one day.** St. Peter is saying that these scoffers and false teachers are using the delay of the Lord to cast doubt on His prophecies, but the concept of time does not exist for God. For God, the word "delay" does not exist because He is above time; He is the one who created time. Time is of no element in the counsels of God. God does not have past, future, or present; everything for Him is present. So, how can I use a term that does not apply to God and use it to cast doubts on the promises of God? The word "delay" does not apply to God. God has eternity and eternity has no beginning and no end, but the concept of time is totally different. He has eternity in which to work out His purposes; God is not under the restraint of time, He is above it. For us who are under the restraint of time, we may consider this as a delay, but for God, He uses this for a certain wisdom. He is giving us opportunity to repent and for our salvation. Thus, what we call, "delay," is a wise counsel from God. He is long suffering and patient, calling more people to repent and be saved.

3:9 **The Lord is not slack concerning His promise, as some count slackness, but is longsuffering toward us, not willing that any should perish but that all should come to repentance.** Delay is not due to slackness, but it is because of the love of God. He is longsuffering, He is patient, He does not wish that even one person would perish. He wants everybody to repent because He does not desire the death of the sinner, but rather that he returns and lives. Here, the false teachers are saying that the Lord did not fulfill His promises, but the true teacher says, "No, this is wisdom from God; it is love, it is kindness, it is compassion, it is longsuffering, and it is patience. He wants us to repent and to return to Him." Therefore, in verses 1 to 9, St. Peter focused on this message—that God's promise is not slack.

3:10 But the day of the Lord will come as a thief in the night. From verses 10 to 13, he speaks about the Day of the Lord. Thus, when we say, "the Day of the Lord," we are speaking about the Day of His Second Coming, when He comes to judge the world in righteousness. St. Peter is saying that the Day of the Lord will come as a thief. Actually, the same words were said by the Lord Jesus Christ as well as by many prophets in the Old Testament. In his mind, St. Peter is comparing between the flood and the Second Coming of the Lord. God waited 120 years with longsuffering and patience, then the flood came as a thief and destroyed the whole world. The Lord Jesus Christ Himself said, "But as the days of Noah were, so also will the coming of the Son of Man be" (Mt 24:37). During the time of Noah, they were eating, drinking, marrying, working, and planting until the flood came and destroyed the whole earth. That is why St. Peter is saying that Day of the Lord "will come as a thief," unexpectedly. While we may not think that He is coming, He will be coming. That is why we need to be watchful for the coming of the Lord.

in which the heavens will pass away with a great noise, and the elements will melt with fervent heat; both the earth and the works that are in it will be burned up. St. Peter now begins to explain how the day of the Lord will look. During the time of Noah, the world was destroyed by water, but in the Second Coming of the Lord, the world will be destroyed by fire. Scientific research proves this to be true, that it will be through fire and explosions that the world will end. St. Peter says, "the heavens will pass away with great noise" (cf. Ps. 102:25, 26; Is. 51:6; Mk 24:35; Mark 13:31; Luke 21:33; [1 Pet. 1:23–25). Of course, he is not speaking about the heaven of heavens, which is the throne of God, but he is speaking about the heavens, which are the earthly heavens—the heavens in relation to the earth, like the clouds, or the firmament in which the birds fly, or space and all the other planets; all these are called "the heavens." These heavens (the whole cosmos, the whole universe) will explode, and that is how the world will end. It is because of these explosions that St. Peter said that the heavens will pass away with great noise. Because of the fires, "the elements will melt with fervent heat; both the earth and the works that are in it will be burned up." The earth and everything on it and in it will be completely burned up with fire and heat.

3:11 Therefore, since all these things will be dissolved. It is a fact, if the Lord said so, then it will happen. "Heaven and earth will pass away," as the Lord said (Mt 24:35). They will be dissolved by fire.

what manner of persons ought you to be in holy conduct and godliness. When a student remembers the day of his exam, he is more serious and more focused on his studies. In the same way, if you remind yourself with the Second Coming of the Lord, that heaven and earth will pass away, if we remind ourselves that we will die and our lives will end, we will live in godliness and holy conduct. I remember once visiting a priest in his office in Cairo, Egypt. I found in the corner of his office that he had put a casket. I asked him, "What is this?" He told me, "This is my casket. I put it here in my office to remind myself that one day I will be in it, standing before the throne of God." This is how serious he was about his life and this is what St. Peter is telling us. That is why every night in the Compline Prayer, the Church reminds us that we will stand before the throne of God: "Behold, I am about to stand before the just judge." Remind yourself and remember that we will stand before the throne of God. If you are lacking zeal, if you are lacking motivation, if you find that the world is keeping you busy, not paying attention to your spiritual life, just think about the Second Coming of the Lord; then, you will conduct your life in holiness and godliness.

3:12 looking for and hastening the coming of the day of God, because of which the heavens will be dissolved, being on fire, and the elements will melt with fervent heat? The Day for the Lord is a day of joy for the righteous, but it is a day of fear and trembling for the wicked. Thus, St. Peter is telling us: "If you live a holy and godly life, you will be looking for the day of the Lord." St. John the Beloved concluded in the Book of Revelation by saying, "Amen. Even so, come, Lord Jesus!" (Rev 22:20), and St. Paul said, "I have the desire to depart and be with Christ, this is much better. For me, to live is Christ, and to die is gain" (Phil 1:21). We should not be afraid of the Day of the Lord, but, rather, we should be looking forward to that day because it is a better life. It is the life from which grief, sorrow, and groaning have fled away. It is a life in which we will be glorified and fully adopted. It is a life in which there is no sin and no hardships. It is a life in which we will be with our beloved God and enjoy being with Him. That is why the righteous are looking forward and hastening to the Day of the Lord. As for the wicked, for them this day is a day of fear; they fear the Day of the Lord because this day will be a day of judgment and condemnation for them. Then St. Peter once more confirms that the world will be destroyed by fire: "because of which the heavens will be dissolved, being on fire." So, this fire will make the heaven melt and dissolve "and the elements of the earth will melt with fervent heat."

3:13 Nevertheless we, according to His promise, look for new heavens and a new earth in which righteousness dwells. Why are we looking for the Second Coming of the Lord? This world is full of wickedness, full of corruption, but the life to come will be a life full of righteousness. That is why He said, "we, according to His promise." God promised us a new earth and a new heaven, so we are looking forward to this new earth and new heaven, "in which righteous dwells," only righteousness. There is no sin, there is no wickedness, there is no corruption—only righteousness. In the Book of Revelation, St. John tells us, "And I saw a new heaven and a new earth," (Rev 21:1). I remember one time asking His Holiness Pope Shenouda III what that means, "a new earth and a new heaven?" The way His Holiness explained it to me is that the place in which we, the believers, dwell will be like earth, compared to the throne of God, which will be like the heaven. It is not a physical earth. It is not a materialistic earth like the earth in which we are living right now, but "a new heaven and a new earth" means the place in which we will dwell, it will be a new, spiritual world—new. By using the words, "earth and heaven," God is speaking to us in our language. How are we to understand what St. Peter means by "earth and heaven?" It means

that earth is our place and heaven is the throne of God. Thus, it will be a new earth and a new heaven because the former heaven and earth will pass away, and the new earth and new heaven will be our place with God. The last verses, from 14 to 17, are the final admonition by St. Peter on how to be steadfast.

3:14 Therefore, beloved, looking forward to these things, be diligent to be found by Him in peace, without spot and blameless. While you are looking forward to the coming of the Lord, to the new heaven and new earth, "be diligent to be found by Him in peace, without spot and blameless."

in peace. As previously noted, only the godly have peace regarding the Day of the Lord. But the ungodly will be anxious regarding the Day of the Lord because this day will be the day of condemnation for them. How will they have peace on the day of their condemnation?

be diligent. You need to take your spiritual life seriously. This reminds me of what he mentions in Chapter 1. In this same epistle, St. Peter says, "Be diligent to add to your faith, you need to add to your faith for it to grow, add to your faith virtue, and add to virtue knowledge, and add to knowledge self-control, and add to self-control perseverance, and add to perseverance godliness, and add to godliness brotherly kindness, and add to brotherly kindness love. You need to add, be diligent to add." So, St. Peter is repeating the same thing here: "If you want to have peace on the Day of the Lord, then be diligent, be serious, grow in your faith, add to your faith."

to be found by Him in peace, without spot and blameless. This reminds me of what St. Paul said in Ephesians, Chapter 5. The Lord died on the cross and left for us His blood and the grace of the Holy Spirit, working in the Mysteries (Sacraments) of the Church. Why? "To present us to Himself a glorious church, without spot or blemish," as we read it in Ephesians 5:27. By saying "without spot and blameless," St. Peter is using the same words St. Paul used in Ephesians, Chapter 5. You need to be found in the Day of the Lord without spot or blemish. Spots are signs of aging. When people grow in age, become old, their bodies become full of spots. The word "blemish" can also be translated to mean "wrinkling," which is also a sign of aging, but as we read in the Old Testament Book of Isaiah, "He renews your life like a youth" (cf. Is 40:31).

He is saying that you need to be diligent to be found like a youth in your spirituality in the Day of the Lord. St. Peter is saying, "I want you to be strong like the eagles (having wings like eagles to fly), not aged, but I want you to be strong like youth, without spot and blameless."

3:15 **and consider that the longsuffering of our Lord is salvation.** What you call a delay is not a delay; it is not slackness. It is an opportunity for you to work on your salvation so that you will be found by Him without spot and blameless, in peace. Do not think that the Lord is slack, but this is His long-suffering for us to work on our salvation.

as also our beloved brother Paul, according to the wisdom given to him, has written to you. He is saying, "These are not my personal words. The words I am telling you, are the words of God. Because it is the same Spirit who inspired me that also inspired St. Paul, so St. Paul also, according to this heavenly wisdom and the inspiration of the Holy Spirit, mentioned to you many times in his epistles about the Day of the Lord." Maybe St. Peter is referring here to the Second Epistle to the Thessalonians because in the First Letter [to the Thessalonians], St. Paul spoke about the Second Coming of the Lord, especially in Chapter 4, so people thought that the Lord is coming right now. That is why in the Second Epistle to the Thessalonians, St. Paul told them, "No, there are signs before the coming of the Lord: 1) The apostasy should happen, which is falling away; 2) The man of sin should be revealed" (cf. 2 Thess 2:3). St Peter is saying, "St. Paul also spoke to you about the Lord not coming immediately. There are signs before His coming. This waiting is not slackness, but it is [God's] longsuffering for us to work on our salvation."

3:16 as also in all his epistles. St. Peter is saying, "In all his epistles, St. Paul spoke about the Second Coming of the Lord." In 1 Corinthians, Chapter 15, St. Paul wrote about the Second Coming of the Lord and about how we should live our lives in holiness and in godliness.

speaking in them of these things. In St. Paul's epistles, he also spoke about the apostasy, like in his Epistle to the Hebrews, for example, where he gave five warnings against apostasy and falling away.

in which are some things hard to understand. This is true. St. Paul's letters are not easy; they are difficult. That is why when we interpret the epistles of St. Paul, we need to interpret them using this rule: comparing spiritual things with spiritual things. We need to interpret them from the Scripture and as the Church Fathers interpreted them. Unfortunately, many denominations were started because of wrong interpretations of St. Paul's letters. For example, salvation by faith only and attacking works is a wrong interpretation of St. Paul's letters, like Romans, Chapter 4, for example. Many denominations, because they interpreted the doctrine and teaching of St. Paul in the wrong way, drifted away from the truth.

which untaught and unstable people twist to their own destruction, as they do also the rest of the Scriptures. "Untaught" means they are untaught by the Holy Spirit, and "unstable" because they changed the teaching that was delivered to us from the Church Fathers, like how some, after the 16th Century, falsely changed the true teaching about Communion; that is instability. A teaching that lasted in the Church for sixteen centuries, that this is the real body and real blood of the Lord Christ Jesus, if I change it after sixteen centuries and deny the reality of the change of the bread and wine into the body and blood of our Lord Jesus Christ, this is instability. St. Peter is makes mention of "untaught" people (those who do not listen to the wisdom of the Holy Spirit and the Church Fathers) and the "unstable" people (those who change the faith that was delivered to the saints), and thus twist right beliefs in a manner that will lead them to their own destruction. They are poor because they do not know that the Scripture that was intended for their own salvation, by their wrong interpretation of it, they will end up using it for their own destruction. Not only the letters of St. Paul, but they also twist the rest of the Scripture. Arius twisted the words of our Lord Jesus Christ when He said, "My Father is greater than I." He twisted this teaching to say that Jesus is not God. That is why St. Peter said, "as they do also the rest of the Scriptures." Here is very, very important advice: Do not rely on your own understanding in interpreting the Scripture. Go to the Church Fathers, go to the Holy Tradition, compare spiritual things with spiritual things, and interpret the Bible by the Bible (in its entirety). Do not take one verse and make a doctrine out of it. Wrong interpretation of the Scripture is very serious. It will end "to their own destruction," as St. Peter said.

3:17 **You therefore, beloved, since you know this beforehand, beware lest you also fall from your own steadfastness.** St. Peter is saying, "Since I told you about the Day of the Lord, that He is not delaying out of slackness but it is out of His longsuffering, His patience, and His mercy, for you to repent and be saved, since you know this beforehand, beware lest you also fall from your own steadfastness, lest you fall from your own stability." Instead, be confirmed in your calling, as he said in Chapter 1 (cf. 2 Pet 1:10), "Make your calling and your election stable. I am warning you lest you follow these false teachers and fall from your steadfastness."

being led away with the error of the wicked. St. Peter calls the false teachers, "the wicked." So, be careful; examine carefully lest you follow a wolf instead of a shepherd. The wolf does not come except to destroy and to kill, but the good shepherd lays His life down for His sheep (cf. Jn 10:11). Beware. If you are led away by the error of false teachers, you will fall from your own steadfastness. Now that you know there are false teachers out there, be careful; be watchful.

3:18 **but grow in the grace and knowledge of our Lord and Savior Jesus Christ.** Again, the message of St. Peter's letters is to encourage us to be diligent in our spiritual growth: grow, add to your faith, and grow in the grace. The grace is a free gift given to us, but we need to grow, which means to use this grace for our growth. Grace is a free gift given to us for what purpose? It is given to us for us to grow in spiritual maturity and to grow in the knowledge of Jesus Christ. Some people only know about the Lord, but St. Peter is telling us, "No, I want you to grow in His knowledge, to know Him, not just to know about Him, but to know Him." As I previously said, this is what makes Christianity different than any other religion. Any other religion is just a set of principles: do this, do not do that, and you do it on your own. However, Christianity is not a set of principles or a set of commandments we need to follow. Christianity is a relationship with Christ, and through this relationship you will be transformed and you will be converted from glory to glory, to His own image and to His own likeness. That is why if you try to keep the Commandments of God without having a relationship with Christ, you will fall and you will fail to, and you do not [even] understand what Christianity is. You will think Christianity is another religion like all these other religions, but Christianity is not just a list of commandments to follow. Christianity is a relationship with God. That is why God came to us and that is why God became Man, for us to enter into this relationship. It is only through this relationship that you will grow, that you will be transformed, and that you will change from image to image, to His likeness. It is impossible to do this outside the relationship. That is why St. Peter told them, "Grow in the grace and knowledge of our Lord and Savior Jesus Christ."

To Him be the glory both now and forever. Amen. St. Peter concludes by a doxology saying, "To Him be the glory both now and forever. Amen." Glory to Him. Glory to Him because He loves us. Glory to Him because He saved us. Glory to Him because He is longsuffering and patient with us. Glory to Him because He does not wish or desire the death of a sinner but rather that he returns and lives. Glory to Him, not only now, but both now, and forever. Amen.

This concludes the Second Epistle of St. Peter in which he reminds us how we need to work diligently on our spiritual growth and spiritual maturity.

Glory be to God forever and ever. Amen.

~~~~~~~~~~

Chapter 3 Questions

1. What is Peter trying to accomplish by writing this second letter?

2. What kind of people will arise in these last days? What will they be led by?

3. What will these people say?

4. Why is God delaying judgment?

5. Because of this kind of judgment, how shall we live?

6. When He comes, what three things should characterize us?

~~~~~~~~~~

www.ingramcontent.com/pod-product-compliance
Lightning Source LLC
LaVergne TN
LVHW061327060426
835511LV00012B/1893